T0116990

fP

WHY PANDAS
DO HANDSTANDS

And Other Curious Truths
About Animals

Augustus Brown

FREE PRESS

New York   London   Toronto   Sydney

FREE PRESS
A Division of Simon & Schuster, Inc.
1230 Avenue of the Americas
New York, NY 10020

Copyright © 2006 by Augustus Brown

Simultaneously published in Great Britain by Transworld Publishers

Published by arrangement with Transworld Publishers,
A Division of The Random House Group Ltd.

FREE PRESS and colophon are trademarks
of Simon & Schuster, Inc.

For information about special discounts for bulk purchases,
please contact Simon & Schuster Special Sales at
1-800-456-6798 or business@simonandschuster.com

DESIGNED BY ERICH HOBBING

Manufactured in the United States of America

1   3   5   7   9   10   8   6   4   2

Library of Congress Cataloging-in-Publication data is available.

ISBN 978-1-4516-2427-4

To Gabriella, Thomas, and Cilene

Contents

PART THREE

THE BIRDS AND THE BEES: ANIMALS
AND THEIR LOVE LIVES   57

PART FOUR

FAMILY AFFAIRS: THE TRIALS AND TRIBULATIONS OF ANIMAL PARENTHOOD 99

PART FIVE

A MATTER OF LIFE AND DEATH: HOW THE FITTEST, STRONGEST, SMARTEST, AND DOWNRIGHT NASTIEST SURVIVE 123

PART SIX

WORK, REST, AND PLAY:
ANIMAL LIFESTYLES   151

PART SEVEN

SOCIAL ANIMAL: HOW CREATURES
LIVE TOGETHER   179

PART ELEVEN
CHILDREN OF THE EVOLUTION:
NATURE'S SUCCESSES AND FAILURES   247

Foreword

Generations ago, even the cleverest people used to dismiss animals as dull, uninteresting creatures—at least compared to us humans.

Mark Twain, for instance, argued that "man is the only animal that blushes, or needs to" while D. H. Lawrence called man "the only animal in the world to fear." G. K. Chesterton, glass in hand no doubt, wrote that "no animal ever invented anything so bad as drunkenness—or as good as drink."

He would have needed a stiff whiskey if he knew how wrong they all had been.

Mr. Chesterton had clearly not encountered a Scandinavian elk, blind drunk on fermented apples, or witnessed the carnage caused when a flock of berry-addled birds fly into the side of a glass tower. Nor, obviously, had Mr. Twain witnessed a sexually aroused male ostrich, its long neck burning a vivid scarlet. If he had, he would have turned bright red himself.

And Mr. Lawrence had obviously never been stung by the awesome Australian box jellyfish. If he had, he would have spent a week suffering from the hideous Irukandji syndrome, a combination of nausea, high blood pressure, and manic depression that can reduce a man to, well, a quivering jelly. If he had, he would have feared animals forever.

In their defense, all three were living in another age, a time before electron microscopes and wildlife filmmakers, the National Geographic channel and computers capable of decoding a dog's DNA.

Today, no one can look at the animal world without feeling amazed on a regular basis.

Every day, or so it seems, a scientific journal or research paper, a wildlife documentary maker, or zoologist is delivering some new discovery or insight. The variety, unpredictability, and pure strangeness of the facts they come up with are endless—and endlessly fascinating: cows produce more milk to the sound of Beethoven; male mice serenade their sweethearts; penguins can fire their feces like cannons; lobsters behave like mobsters; elephants can imitate the sound of passing trucks. Animal life, clearly, is anything but dull.

This book is an assembly of some of the curious, the bizarre, and the sometimes barely credible things we now know about animals.

As will be obvious from the beginning, this is a collection intended to inform and educate, but, above all, to entertain. So, while I have been scrupulous in providing source references and have endeavored to maintain scientific accuracy at every turn, I have not let pedantry get in the way of the sense of fun and wonder that, I hope, lies at the book's heart.

To have done so would have been to risk making animals uninteresting to another generation. And that simply wouldn't do.

—Augustus Brown, London, 2006

PART ONE

TALK TO THE ANIMALS:
THE CURIOUS ART
OF ANIMAL COMMUNICATION

The best thing about animals is that they don't talk much.

—Thornton Wilder,
The Skin of Our Teeth

In truth, it's a wonder we can hear ourselves think. Animals everywhere are deep in conversation, chattering away about food, sex, and child care, transmitting top-secret messages about homeland security or just gossiping idly about passing strangers.

And all in a range of ingenious, often bizarre, languages. Creatures hum and drum, sing and dance their news. They use semaphore signals and color codes, release chemical smells and secretions. Almost anything, its seems, constitutes talk to the animals—even breaking wind.

Body Talk:
How Animals Use Their Anatomies
to Communicate

Herring communicate by breaking wind.

They produce high-frequency bursts of sound by releasing air from their anuses. This also produces a stream of fine bubbles that is visible to other herring.

Herring do this primarily during darkness and when there are high numbers of fish around. Scientists think they can hear the sounds and are communicating with each other about their location. Researchers have named the herring language Fast Repetitive Tick, or FRT for short.

*

Snakes emit a flatulent pop to scare off their enemies. A scientist studying two breeds of snake from the southwestern United States, the Sonoran coral snake and the western hook-nosed snake, heard them emitting a rumble from their cloaca, the opening at the rear used for sex and excretion. He concluded the noise was being generated by air bubbles and was the first evidence of snake flatulence.

*

Crayfish have a quick and effective way of warning each other of danger. At the first sign of a predator they simply empty their bladders.

Lobsters have taken this language a step further: they communicate by urinating in each other's faces. The urine is fired from tiny jets near the lobster's eyes and is laced with chemicals that transmit messages, mainly about flirting or fighting.

*

Chipmunks also relay important information to each other by urinating. Their signaling system is sophisticated enough for them to be able to mark not only spots where there is food, but also places where all the supplies have been eaten.

*

Voles are another species that communicate with each other by marking their environment with urine. Unfortunately, this isn't the safest form of communication given that their most prolific predators are birds of prey like kestrels. The vole's urine is visible in ultraviolet light and a kestrel has the ability to see using UV vision. Unsurprisingly, voles suffer massive falls in population when kestrels pay attention to their movements.

*

Scientists believe elephants communicate with each other by transmitting vibrations through the earth. By making the ground rumble with a series of stamps and mock charges, the six-ton creatures can relay messages as far as 20 miles away, much farther than airborne sound travels. The messages are then picked up by other elephants, via their feet, which act as their antennae. Scientists have described seeing elephants running in the opposite direction when other elephants were being slaughtered miles away. They think that the fleeing elephants were alerted to the threat by the foot stamping of their dying herd members.

African elephants are also capable of learning to imitate sounds. Scientists have recorded them imitating, among other things, the sound of trucks passing on nearby highways. Why they do this is, at the moment, unclear.

*

Kangaroos communicate with their tails.

If a member of a group of red kangaroos spots a predator they will either stamp their feet or use their large, heavy tail to pound the earth. This is the signal for the rest of the group to scatter and leave the dominant male to defend them from the attacker.

Kangaroos also make a small number of noises. Red kangaroos click, for instance, while gray female kangaroos cluck when calling their young. Coughs can be a signal of submission when two males are fighting.

*

The golden frog, a rare amphibian from Costa Rica and Panama, has its own version of semaphore language. It makes slow, circular movements with its front and hind limbs that signal to other frogs the direction it is taking. Researchers think the frogs are communicating messages that include "I'm coming towards you" and "I'm going to take care of you."

*

Cuttlefish wink. The fish change the patterns on their back according to their mood and have two black eye spots that they can manipulate to signal their presence.

Vocal Heroes:
Birds, Whales, and Other Singing Stars

Scientists think birds use the same combinations of notes, rhythms, and pitch permutations as we do.

When researchers slowed down recordings of the birdsong of two species of wren they were surprised to discover they were singing classical music. A white-breasted wood wren produced the familiar "da da da daaaaah" of Beethoven's *Fifth Symphony,* while a canyon wren sang a trilling cascade of notes that almost exactly echoed the opening of Chopin's *Revolutionary Étude.* Whether or not the composers drew inspiration from birds is unclear, but Mozart, at least, was willing to give credit to his pet starling for inspiring him. When the bird sang his new *Piano Concerto in G Major* back to him, with the sharps changed to flats, Mozart admitted it was an improvement and incorporated the starling's changes.

Birds produce many of the sounds made by human orchestral instruments. The song of the Australian diamond firetail finch, for example, sounds like an oboe. The sound of the white-bellied green imperial pigeon or the strawberry finch could easily be mistaken for a flute. The potoo sings like a bassoon, while the western crowned pigeon from New Guinea woos its mates with notes that could be produced by a tuba.

*

Two of the best mimics in the bird kingdom are myna birds and the Australian lyrebird, each of whom can perfectly imitate the songs of other birds. But the title of champion mimic probably belongs to the mockingbird. While observing a male northern mockingbird over a year or so, one bird-watcher heard it mimic the sound of twenty-five other birds, from gulls and sparrow hawks, to blackbirds and thrushes. Some claim to have heard it imitating other sounds, from a creaky door to a cat's meow.

Ornithologists think the mockingbird's gifts are a means of attracting members of the opposite sex. Females are drawn to males with the biggest repertoire because it is a sign of their fitness as mates. The females may also think if they know so much about other birds, they will also know where they keep their food supplies.

*

The nightingale may have nature's best musical ear. It can repeat complicated pieces of music containing 60 different "phrases." The nightingale's singing abilities are also exceptional. Its repertoire includes 900 different types of melody.

*

Male birds sing in the morning to appear more macho. Birds tend to gorge during the day, then fast at night so, in theory, they should be at their weakest in the morning. By delivering a lusty dawn chorus, a male sends out the message that he is still full of energy.

Some species of birds break into song earlier in the day

than others. Blackbirds and song thrushes, for instance, can strike up their dawn chorus more than an hour and a half before birds like chaffinches and blue tits. Scientists have found that the bigger the bird's eyes the sooner it strikes up a song. Singing not only attracts mates but predators, like owls, too. With their hearing out of action while they warble, they have to be able to rely on their eyes to see any attacks coming. Those with smaller eyes need extra sunlight to be sure of their safety.

*

Birds pass on songs from generation to generation. Tropical wrens do this on a gender basis. Fathers pass on their repertoires of chirps and tweets to their sons, mothers give theirs to their daughters.

Female songbirds learn faster than males. A study showed that a female cardinal was able to learn a selection of music in one-third of the time it took a male to learn the same number of songs.

*

A rare South American bird barks like a dog.

Ornithologists who discovered the bird, known as the Jocotoco antpitta, in southern Ecuador in 1997 think it makes the bizarre call to warn of intruders entering its territory.

*

Birds band together to sing triumphant songs when they win territorial fights.

When the tropical boubou from the Ivory Coast succeeds in driving an invader from its neighborhood, pairs of the birds perform distinctive duets to signal their victory. Researchers think the call lets other boubous know the coast is clear and also warns off other potential intruders.

*

Owls hoot less when it rains. Wet weather acts as a dampener on the acoustics within woodland and forests. Owls' calls are 70 times more likely to be heard when it is dry.

*

Loony tunes aren't funny. The male loon has a distinctive song, a loud yodel that is a clear threat to other birds. According to one scientist, it is translated as "come near me and I'll pull all your feathers out." Unusually, loons also radically change their tunes when they move to a new home. They do so, apparently, to make sure they sound different to the birds already living there. Again, this is a signal that they are not to be messed with, that there is, you might say, a dark side to the loon.

*

Male bronze-winged jacanas live in a harem ruled by the female of the species. The birds yell when they want to compete for her attention.

*

What you eat affects your singing voice, at least if you are a bird. Just like musical instruments, different shaped beaks produce different sounds. Heavy beaks, designed to crush tough seeds, make deeper, less complicated sounds than slim beaks, which are ideal for snatching insects. So birds with heavy beaks can't produce the same range or trill as fast as those with smaller beaks.

*

The North American black-capped chickadee, named after its famous call, uses a system of warning cries, graded to indicate the level of threat its flock faces. The soft, high-pitched "seet" sound warns of airborne predators, such as owls and hawks, and tells the other chickadees to take cover and stay in place until an "all clear" call comes. A full "chick a dee" warns of a resting predator, such as an owl perched on a tree branch. When chickadees hear this call, they flock together and crowd the predator until it flies away, sometimes joined by other birds such as nuthatches and small woodpeckers who also recognize the signal. The most serious alarm call is, however, reserved for small raptors that the chickadee would find hard to evade, such as pygmy owls. This time the "chick a dee" call is punctuated with several extra "dees" at the end. This tells the flock to scatter.

*

The deepest-voiced bird is the cassowary, and, after the ostrich, the world's largest. It uses low-frequency infrasound, only used by one other land-living animal, the elephant. Its call can be pitched as low as 23 Hertz (Hz), the bottom of the range we can hear as humans.

*

Humpback whales can sing continuously for up to twenty-four hours at a time. Whales can sing over a range of at least seven octaves. Yet the intervals between the notes are similar to those humans use in musical scales. As a result, their song is made up of rhythms and patterns that are identical to some human musical forms, from ballads to classical sonatas. Scientists have concluded that they are constantly composing new themes to attract admirers. The male humpback whale is the most inventive song-writer, specializing in songs with what sound like rhyming lyrics.

The low-frequency pulse of the blue whale can be as loud as 188 decibels—that is noisier than a jet engine. They can be picked up from as far as 500 miles away.

Fin whales can communicate with each other when they are 2,000 miles apart.

Male dwarf minke whales make a very different sound, however. The distinctive *ba-ba-boinnnnnnggg* noise sounds like a laser gun and has been nicknamed the Star Wars call. It is believed the minke whale uses the noise to keep other whales at a distance.

Killer whales use different dialects to communicate with each other.

Like pop music, whale song can move in and out of fashion. When whales off the Pacific coast of Australia encountered a stray school from the Indian Ocean coast of the same continent, they were immediately taken by the visitors' collection of songs. Within a year the east coast whales had dropped their old tunes and adopted the Indian Ocean songbook.

Mystery surrounds the most unusual of all whale songs. It has been heard in the oceans since 1992 and doesn't match the song patterns of any known whale. It is also pitched at a frequency of 52 Hz, well above the normal 15-to-20-Hz frequency of other whales. The whale's migration patterns are unique, too, leading some scientists to speculate it is an undiscovered species of the mammal.

*

Fish sing. Male plainfin midshipmen hum at nighttime to attract females. Their songs are so distinctive they are also known as Californian singing fish. Juvenile fish aren't able to hum, however. They can only grunt.

Dolphins whistle. Each dolphin has its own signature sound, which allows it to be recognized by others. They are also gifted mimics and can imitate each other's whistles. They use this skill to communicate with unfamiliar dolphins in the wild.

*

The phrase "quiet as a mouse" is misleading as mice do much more than let out the occasional squeak. A study of male mice discovered that they reacted to the sexual smells of female mice by emitting ultrasonic sounds. When scientists slowed these sounds down, they found they were songs. They concluded the mice were serenading their potential partners.

Rats whistle secretly to each other. The rodents produce the ultrasonic sound from deep inside their throats. The whistle's frequency ensures it is only picked up by fellow rats and doesn't tip off potential prey that they are about to pounce.

*

Some frogs have a song in their throat. A talented species of Chinese frog can perform an amazing range of vocal acrobatics, belting out everything from apelike growls and birdsong to low-frequency songs similar to those sung by whales. The frog owes its amazing versatility to having two pairs of vocal sacs rather than the usual one.

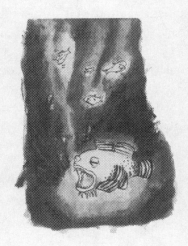

Female frogs and crickets select their partners on a first-come-first-served basis. So, male frogs and crickets all sing at the same time because they are afraid of missing out on an available female. They also call out as fast as they can, which produces the often deafening frog or cricket chorus.

The North American bullfrog has a particularly booming voice, mainly because it uses its ears as amplifiers.

*

Less naturally gifted creatures make their own amplifiers.

Male mole crickets serenade females from the burrows they dig in the sand. They dig the burrows with horn-shaped openings which amplify the sound, especially when wet. Other species of crickets cut leaves to amplify their calls.

*

Frogs can also play woodwind. A species from the rain forest of Borneo has been discovered using a tree in which it lives as a musical instrument. While wooing females, the males sit half-submerged in water-filled cavities in the trees' trunks. As they boom out their calls, they adjust the pitch and length of their notes until they hit a frequency that resonates with the tree, amplifying the sound they are making, rather like a human humming in the shower until he or she finds the resonant frequency. Scientists think the frogs do this to sound even sexier to potential mates. They know of no other animal that effectively plays a musical instrument in this way.

*

Spiny lobsters can play themselves like violins. The lobsters draw the protrusions at the bottom of their antenna—known as plectra—across a set of ridges under their eyes when they feel threatened or want to object to something. The action is very similar to a violinist drawing a bow across a string. The noise acts as an alarm or protest signal.

*

Woodchucks, also known as groundhogs, use a whistling sound to warn one another of danger. Hence their nickname of the whistling pig.

*

The New Guinea singing dog is unique. As well as yelping and barking, like other dogs, it emits a series of cries that are a mixture of birdcalls and whale song.

The Anthills Are Alive:
How Animals Buzz, Bang, Bounce,
and Rap

Music is everywhere in the insect world with many species vibrating their wings to produce a rhythmic buzz. The housefly, for instance, creates a hum by beating its wings at 345 strokes per second producing a middle octave pitch of F. Queen honeybees make a range of sounds, including quacking and tooting noises, the former announcing the presence of challengers in the nest. Another bee, the melipona, uses a buzzing "Morse code" to guide the rest of its hive to sources of food.

Many animals communicate by sending vibrations to each other. Among those who pass on good and bad vibes are frogs, chameleons, and termites. The most impressive sound may be that made by a Costa Rican stinkbug. Males work together to send tremors through plant leaves that are then translated into an airborne sound, very similar to the distinctive melody of a tuba.

*

Ants have different forms of music. Drumming, or body rapping, is common in species who live in wood or dried-pulp nests. Ants bang their front mandibles and their rear ends against the wall of the nest in bursts of seven thumps, at 50-millisecond intervals.

*

Caterpillars tap-dance. Biologists believe the butterfly caterpillars do the dance on leaves and plant stems to attract ants which protect them from predatory wasps.

Honeybees also communicate by dancing. They do a waggle dance to let other bees know how far away and in which direction they need to travel to locate food. Another dance, in which they tremble, signals to bees that they should not fly off for more nectar because there is too much arriving at the hive. The honeybee also communicates by increasing its body heat when it finds food.

*

Blind mole rats communicate with each other by drumming their heads against the roofs of their tunnels. The drumming produces a seismic reaction that other mole rats can understand. Scientists suspect the rats also use their drumming to measure the distances they have tunnelled.

*

Bees buzz less during hot weather. The honeybee slows down the rate at which it beats its wings so as to cool its body down and reduce the risk of overheating.

*

The knocking sound of the notorious deathwatch beetle, which eats its way through timber, is in fact a form of sexual communication.

*

Butterflies make threats in Morse code.

Scientists heard blue and white longwing butterflies make a series of clicking sounds when they confronted a different species of butterfly. As well as directing the clicks at the other butterflies, the longwings used them to communicate with each other.

Hot Gossip:
What Animals Talk About

Prairie dogs chat about passing strangers. The rodents have a highly developed language with special words to warn against the threat of different animals.

Scientists at Northern Arizona University decoded the prairie dogs' calls into a collection of key signals. These signals included a single sharp note meaning "hawk overhead," repeated calling by a group to signal "coyote alert," and a mix of long notes and barks to indicate "human approaching."

They also found that prairie dogs can get carried away while making their territorial call, which they deliver while standing on their hind legs. Prairie dogs can get so excited they leap into the air, flip over, and fall backwards.

The most intriguing discovery, however, was that prairie dogs have calls for animals that pose no threat to them, such as cows. They also created a new call for a wooden object that scientists dragged across the desert near their colony. The scientists concluded that along with looking out for each other, the highly sociable rodents like to chat about the world as it passes by their front doors.

*

Chimpanzees talk about food. A study at Edinburgh Zoo found chimps used different high- and low-pitched grunts to communicate about different foods. The high-pitched sound was associated with bread, which they liked. The low-pitched groan was for apples, of which they weren't so fond.

*

Female baboons talk about sex. And the better it was for them, the more noise they make about it. The females make a series of loud, machine-gun-like grunts after mating. Some biologists believe the chatter is linked to the quality of intercourse with the male partner—the higher his status, the more intense the noise. They think it is the female's way of giving the superior sperm the best chance of fertilizing her eggs. It deters other males and perhaps even swells the male's pride so that he protects her.

*

Some types of ants squeak by performing a routine called stridulation in which they rub together two different parts of their hindmost body section. This produces a high-pitched rasping sound. Scientists have observed ants using this to signal different things. Leaf-cutter ants have been known to squeak an emergency call to summon help when a nest has caved in. Females also use it to stop mating, indicating their sperm-storage system is at full capacity.

*

Dogs' barks vary according to the situations they face. Noisy, low-pitched, or harsh barks are common when a dog feels threatened, insecure, or in physical distress. Barks become more frequent the more threatened a dog feels. When dogs feel happier, for instance playing or acting submissively, their barks are more musical and high-pitched.

*

Llamas have a reputation as quiet creatures, but in fact they make a range of sounds to communicate with each other. Their main means of communicating is humming. Different hums convey different emotions. If they are hot, tired, or uncomfortable, the hum is soft and drawn out, a little like a groan. If they are curious the hum is shorter and higher pitched. A longer, high-pitched hum indicates they are worried or distressed about something. Finally, mother llamas also produce a smooth, medium-pitched hum to soothe their offspring, or cria.

Llamas can also deliver a strange alarm call. One llama expert described it as sounding like a cross between a turkey call and a car engine trying to start.

Sex, predictably, has another range of sounds. When flirting they can make a clucking sound, similar to a person clicking their tongue. Males will make a sound similar to a human gargling when aroused. This noise continues while mating, which can go on for an hour.

In addition to these vocal sounds, llamas have another method of getting messages across to each other. If one llama is unhappy with another llama it will spit at it. Spitting is a last resort, however. Their saliva carries the foul smell and taste of rotting rubbish because llamas are ruminants like cows. The taste left in their mouth after spitting is so unpleasant, llamas keep their mouths open for a few minutes afterwards to get rid of the terrible stench.

*

Vervet monkeys have different calls to indicate they are being attacked by snakes, eagles, or leopards. If it is the first of these, they check their neighborhood for the intruder. If it is the second, they scan the skies and drop out of the trees. If it is the latter, they scramble up into the trees.

*

Cockroaches have a hissing language.

A species of the insect from Madagascar produces a hissing sound by expelling air through a pair of breathing holes, or spiracles, on their abdomens. Males have the greater range of hisses, communicating with other roaches via four different sounds varying in pattern and strength. They have a special hiss they use during courtship and another one for territorial disputes with other males. Females mainly hiss in disapproval when they are disturbed.

*

Squirrels don't listen to cohorts who overreact. A study of one species, the Richardson's ground squirrel, discovered that the animals responded differently to alarm calls from fellow squirrels. Scientists found that the squirrels paid less attention to those with a history of raising false alarms.

*

Pandas make a variety of noises. They can bleat, squeak, moan, growl, bark, and honk.

*

Scientific studies of cat sounds have unearthed a subtle language that is used for different situations, conveying a range of emotions. A murmur is a request or greeting, while a purr is a social sound normally indicating submission. Growls and hisses, predictably, are associated with antagonistic situations, while shrieks signal aggression or pain. Hisses can also be followed by another sound, a short, explosive spit.

Cats chatter their teeth when they hunt or, more commonly, when they are actively prevented from hunting. They yawn as a reaction to smells they don't recognize. Finally, cats make squeaking sounds during play and in anticipation of mealtimes. Females also squeak after sex.

The Power of Speech:
Animals with Spectacular Voices

Dolphins can bray like donkeys. The bottle-nosed dolphins probably make the noise as a tactic to stop prey in their tracks.

*

King cobras growl.

*

Caterpillars can roar. Hook-tip caterpillars are highly territorial and create a din when others invade their space. The insect raps, rasps, and scrapes against the leaves of its home with its jaw and other body parts. If the invader is another caterpillar the two insects may have a shouting match.

In insect terms the caterpillar roar must be frightening. In a quiet environment, scientists have heard the sound from a distance of up to 16 feet. It must also be effective. Most caterpillars who make this noise to eject invading insects retain territorial control of their homes.

*

Several animals can lay claim to having the most dramatic call. The mating cry the male toadfish makes while underwater, for instance, is so powerful it can be heard by humans above water. Cheetahs make a chirping sound, similar to a bird's chirp or a dog's yelp. The sound is so intense, it can be heard a mile away. The most piercing noise on land, however, is almost certainly created by the howler monkey whose ear-splitting call can be heard three miles away.

A cicada can be heard from a quarter of a mile away.

Perhaps the most spectacular sound in all the animal world is that of the snapping shrimp. Only an inch and a half long, the shrimp can use its single large claw to make a snap so loud it sounds like a firecracker. The sound can stun or even kill the shrimp's prey, such is its power. Scientists have discovered that the intensity of the sound is from the way the shrimp snaps the bubbles that collect inside the closing claw.

*

Tigers communicate via a sophisticated range of sounds. To signal to each other, the big cats growl, hiss, and purr, often at frequencies humans can't hear. By far the most effective tool in their acoustic vocabulary, however, is the roar they use to intimidate predators. Studies have found this is delivered at a frequency below 20 Hz, an infrasound signal that is capable of permeating buildings and even mountains. Because of this, a tiger's roar can carry over long distances, up to 1.2 miles. Its most dramatic effect, however, is on those at the receiving end of it. The roar physically rattles and then paralyzes the recipient with fear.

*

The oddest-sounding fish is the Atlantic croaker, which vibrates muscles against its swim bladder to make a drumlike call. It sounds more like a frog than a fish, hence its name. Why croakers croak when and where they do remains a mystery.

*

The African, or cape penguin, which lives on the South African coast, makes a sound unlike any other member of its animal family—a donkey's bray, hence its nickname: the jackass penguin.

The Joy of Rex:
How Dogs and Other Animals
Show They're Happy

Laughter is common to many species, not just humans. Rats at play chirp with joy.

Dogs laugh by panting. Man's best friends make a distinctive breathing noise that to the human ear sounds like the normal, breathless panting a dog makes after exercise. But closer analysis of recordings revealed that when dogs make this sound they exhale in a wider range of frequencies than during normal panting. Scientists believe this is a dog's way of signaling to other dogs it is in a happy and playful mood.

*

Ice-skating buffaloes emit excited noises. They have been observed sliding across frozen surfaces, letting out a joyous "gwaaa" as they go.

*

The horse "laugh" is nothing of the sort. Male horses, zebras, and other relatives curl up their top lips to heighten their sense of smell, particularly during the mating season when they need to assess whether a female is ready to mate. This is known as the Flehmen response.

Dress Code:

What Animals Wear, and What It Tells Other Animals About Them

Much like the military, wasps rank each other by their stripes. The distinctive yellow and black stripes on their abdomens, along with the colored blotches on their faces, convey to wasps where each individual fits into the strict hierarchy of their nest.

*

Chameleons not only change skin color to blend in with their surroundings, but also to communicate with each other. Males become more brightly marked to advertise their dominance, while females become dark or flash red spots to show they are not interested in sex. The darker they get, the more aggressive they are in rejecting potential partners.

*

Humans fly a white flag of surrender, salmon display a dark one. Young Atlantic salmon signal submission by darkening the spots on their bellies when sparring with each other.

*

Butterflies color code themselves. Butterfly caterpillars protect themselves from being eaten by birds by ingesting

noxious chemicals from plants. When they metamorphose into butterflies they advertise their poisonous state
by carrying specific colors on their wings. Birds then
know to avoid them at all costs. Butterflies in the same
neighborhood share information on which colors denote
danger and stick to the same color coding.

*

Wasps must wear wax "uniforms." They smear themselves with the wax from their nest so fellow wasps know
they come from the same colony. If they leave and return
without the wax coating they will be attacked, stung, and
driven from the nest.

*

Having a yellow streak is no bad thing, in one bird species
at least. Male blue tits that have yellow feathers on their
breasts tend to be good providers for their chicks. Female
blue tits prefer these yellowbellies as a result.

*

A species of bird, the siskin, can tell which of its brethren to
share its food with simply by looking at their chest feathers.
Studies have shown that the bigger the black patch on the
chest, the hungrier the bird will tend to be. The patches also
signal status within the siskin community.

*

In one finch community redheads rule the roost.

The rare Australian Gouldian finch has a head that
comes in one of only three colors: red, yellow, or black.
Studies showed that male redheads are the most aggressive. Yellow and black birds are afraid to challenge them,
so the red birds always sit at the top of the pecking order.

*

The size of a female baboon's bottom signals how good she is as a mother. The bigger and more swollen the backside, the greater the baboon's physical prowess as a child bearer.

*

Animals use chemicals to raise the alarm. If a minnow is bitten by a predator, for instance, a substance released into the water from its broken skin will alert other members of its community to avoid the area for hours afterwards. Other species of fish may also pick up on the chemical, which scientists think produces a sense of fear in the animals that detect it. Snails, earthworms, and sea urchins are among the other species known to produce similar warning chemicals.

*

Friends, elephants, countrymen, lend me your ears. Elephants use secretions from glands behind their ears as a form of chemical communication.

Young male elephants smell of honey, at least for part of the year. Male elephants' interest in sex becomes heightened several times each year when they enter a state called musth. During this period, competition between males is intense and often violent. Mature males secrete a pungent brown liquid from a gland between their eye and ear to signal they are available and ready to mate with a female. The young, sexually immature males release the sweet, honey-like secretion to let the older males know they are not interested in competing for females and are therefore no threat to them.

PART TWO

CREATURE COMFORTS:
FOOD AND DRINK
IN THE ANIMAL KINGDOM

In the natural world you are what—or more likely who—you eat. Which in the case of rats and cockroaches means you may well be your closest relative.

Not all animals are opportunistic omnivores, however. Some stick to diets that are high in salt or sugar, others crave food that is rich in blood or fat (sucked fresh from their victim's brain, if possible). And while there are those animals for whom fast food is the only option, there are others who can enjoy the luxury of a long, extremely filling lunch. Then, of course, there are animals who like drugs and alcohol, a combination that generally spells one thing: trouble.

You Are Who You Eat:
Who's Eating Who in the Animal World

Animals really are what they eat. Flamingos are not naturally pink in color. Their distinctive pigmentation comes from their food, tiny green algae, which turn pink during the digestive process. Shrimp, too, lend them their distinctive hue.

*

You are as deadly as what you eat, too. Poison frogs have glands in their skin that exude secretions so toxic that a tiny smear can kill a horse. The frogs brew the poison inside them by eating a diet of toxic insects.

*

Animals can learn to stomach almost anything, however. The monarch butterfly protects itself from predators by releasing poisonous chemicals that can result in a swift and painful death if it is eaten. However, Mexican mice have become immune to the poison and feast on the butterflies each winter.

*

Insects can naturally eat almost anything without suffering any harm because of their superefficient "kidney," which can flush toxins and other harmful substances through their system.

*

Koalas are famous for living on a diet of eucalyptus leaves. But they do grow bored with the fragrant leaves occasionally and drop out of their homes in the eucalyptus tree to eat soil and gravel. However, as a young baby, the koala's first solid meal is altogether different. They eat their mother's droppings. The feces are filled with microbes that will help immunize them against disease and aid their digestion.

*

Vampire bats have the most boring diet in the world. While drinking nothing but blood might be repetitive it does have the advantage of saving them from having to choose food. Unlike virtually every other species, vampires don't bother learning to avoid foods that might make them sick. In any case, there is an easy way of spotting if blood is toxic—its owner is probably dead.

Bats aren't the only vampires. An East African spider has an acquired taste for human blood. It specifically targets blood-sucking mosquitoes knowing that they feed off the blood of humans and other mammals. And on the Galapagos Islands, birds attack other larger birds to drink their blood. The small finches resort to behaving like vampires during the dry season.

The lamprey is the marine world's equivalent of the vampire. The eellike fish hunts trout and other smaller species. Once it has its target in sight it sinks its teeth into the trout's soft tissue and begins sucking out its body fluids.

*

Some moths live off the tears of other animals. Among the animals that sustain the moths are crying cattle, deer, horses, tapirs, pigs, and elephants. In southeast Asia moths feed off the dewy eyes of water buffalo.

*

Cannibalism is rife in the animal world with creatures from birds to frogs, rats to apes, capable of eating members of their own species, particularly when they are young or in egg form. Indeed some species, such as frogs, breed extra eggs specifically so that their offspring can eat them if necessary.

Salamander embryos, for instance, eat their fellow embryos while still in the womb.

Cockroaches will also eat anything, including each other. The Oriental cockroach does have favorite foods, however. It particularly likes sugary or starchy food.

*

Spadefoot toad tadpoles are careful not to eat their relatives.

These tadpoles are cannibals and develop powerful jaws in order to munch other tadpoles. But before eating their meal they carry out a quick chemical taste test to make sure they are not related. If, by some accident, they do swallow a brother or sister they will recognize this taste and spit it out.

*

Cannibalism is good for snails. A study found that young snails who ate their siblings and other unhatched snails lived longer than those who didn't.

Acquired Tastes:
Some Animal Likes
and Dislikes

The kea, a relative of the parrot, is nature's only known rubber fetishist.

The kea is known as a maverick bird with a maverick appetite. It often attacks sheep at night, pecking at their hindquarters to get through the fleece then going on into the fatty areas around the kidneys, eventually killing the sheep.

But it is its strange taste for rubber that has made it the subject of folklore in its native New Zealand. Stories abound of kea pecking away at the rubber of the windshield wipers on various vehicles. They will hang on even if the vehicle is moving and will only release their grip on the wipers when the driver accelerates past 40 miles per hour.

The most dramatic story, however, involves a car left outside overnight. Its owner returned to find that a mob of kea had eaten all the rubber surrounding the windshield. As a result the glass had fallen into the car. The kea, also known for their taste for foam rubber, had ripped open all the seats, pulling out all the foam, and then gone on to trash the car.

*

Geese are partial to polystyrene. In 2005 a flock ate their way through the polystyrene walls of an entire school in the Romanian village of Risesti.

Termites like eating plastic garbage bags.

*

Chimpanzees crave fat-filled meals and eat other monkeys in order to get one. In Tanzania and the Ivory Coast, hunter chimps prey on colobus monkeys in particular. When they catch a colobus, the chimps consume the monkey's brain first. It contains the densest source of fat. They then move on to suck out the fatty marrow from the colobus's longest bones. Only then will they go on to the meat. What they don't eat the hunter chimps share with their friends. Females who join them on the hunt will only get some meat if they agree to have sex.

Polar bears also live on a diet of fat. Such is their craving for lipid-rich food, they will kill a seal pup purely to eat its highly fatty brain.

*

Crickets love salt. Studies have shown that their desire for salty snacks, such as earth soaked in urine, is a key influence in driving swarms of crickets to march. They are also partial to protein snacks, such as seed pods, flowers, and mammal feces.

Elephants eat huge quantities of salt and even go mining for it. An extinct volcano on the border of Kenya and Uganda has been mined extensively for its supplies of minerals. Scientists believe they contain salts the elephants can't get from the soil. The elephants pick their way 1,150 feet up a dangerous track to get to the mines.

*

Chimps have a sweet tooth. They choose fruit, leaves, and bark that contain a high level of glucose, sucrose, and fructose.

Some lizards have a sweet tooth. A Balearic lizard that lives on a small island off Minorca drinks nectar like a bee.

The American and Canadian red squirrel gets through the winter by creating its own supply of maple syrup. When the squirrel's stores of pinecones and nuts run out, it scores the bark of sugar maple trees with its sharp teeth, allowing the sap to drain. When the sap has dried in the sun it leaves a sugary residue, which the squirrel licks to get a valuable boost of energy.

*

Cats don't like sweets. They can't taste them.

Researchers have discovered that all members of the feline family, from the domestic cat to the leopard and the lion, have a strong dislike for sugary foods. By analyzing the cat's genetic code they learned that part of the code that normally provides an animal with sweet taste receptors is missing. This has left cats simply unable to detect sweet-tasting compounds like sugars and carbohydrates. This would explain why cats are keener on savory tastes like meat. And it would also explain why they are, in the wild, among nature's most expert hunters.

*

Chocolate can kill dogs.

The theobromine present in chocolate is toxic and stimulates the cardiac and nervous systems to a dangerous extent, especially in smaller pups. Dogs can experience vomiting, hyperexcitability, and shaking. In severe cases a dog can die from a heart attack. Dark baking chocolate is the most dangerous form of chocolate to dogs as it contains six to seven times the amount of theobromine as plain milk chocolate.

*

Mosquitoes carrying malaria are more likely to be drawn to sweet tastes. The presence of the parasite in their system sends them on a sugar binge.

Only female mosquitoes bite. They are attracted to, among other things, human sweat.

Eating Disorders:
How Some Animals Starve
and Others Binge

The phrase "to eat like a bird" is a misnomer. The vulture, for instance, eats up to a quarter of its body weight in a single feed. Sometimes it can't get back into the air afterwards, and it has to vomit much of its digested food in order to make a quick takeoff. The flamingo rarely overindulges like this, however, even if it hasn't eaten for weeks. It can only eat slowly with its head upside down.

*

Hummingbirds eat almost constantly.

The tiny bird is the avian kingdom's equivalent of a helicopter crossed with a Harrier jump jet. It is capable of flying backwards, flapping its wings 90 times per second while hovering and twice that rate when diving. But the energy it uses up in doing this means it has to constantly stoke its engines with food. Each day the hummingbird must eat more than its body weight in food—and not just any old food either. Because it burns calories at such a high rate, it must have a diet of high-energy nectar. Given its need to get as much energy as possible as quickly as possible it eats fast, too. A hummingbird can extract up to 12 slurps of nectar per second.

*

One of the animal kingdom's ultimate fast food eaters is the Australian thorny devil, a spiky ant-eating lizard. The tiny ants the devil feeds on offer pitifully low amounts of nutrition, so it needs to eat as many as it can as quickly as it can to survive. The thorny devil catches ants by flicking out its tongue at lightning speed, then simply swallows its meal whole without chewing. This allows it to eat an average of 2,000 ants per day.

*

The elephant is one of the most impressive eaters in the animal kingdom. It can consume between 220 and 660 pounds of food and up to 50 gallons of water per day.

A large swarm of locusts can eat 20,000 tons of corn in a day.

The female flea consumes 15 times her own body weight in blood every day.

Moles are capable of eating their own weight in earthworms every day.

Blue whales eat between 1.5 and 3 tons of food per day while feeding. That is the equivalent of 8,000 hamburgers.

*

Orca whales eat a wide range of animals, from fish to seals, penguins and turtles to shark and even blue whales. They can eat a baby seal or sea lion whole.

Whales have different techniques for eating. Some use their teeth, and some strain their food through whalebone filters. A rare family, beaked whales, however, are toothless and have giant lips with a tiny opening at the end of their beak. They can only suck.

*

Squirrels gorge themselves on nuts until they swell up in size. A squirrel that squeezed through the metal mesh of a bird feeder in Devon found it couldn't get back out on its own.

*

Taking a drink of water is a perilous business for a giraffe. To do so it has to splay its legs apart and lower its neck carefully into the water. This makes the giraffe an easy target for predators like lions so it often goes weeks without drinking. Instead it gets moisture from plants such as acacia leaves.

Baboons in the Namib Desert of southern Africa, one of the driest places on earth, can apparently go without water for up to 26 days.

Cockroaches can live without food for one month, but will only survive two weeks without water.

Calls of Nature:
Some Unpleasant Truths
About Animal Bodily Functions

Tree-dwelling sloths store their waste for a week at a time during the dry seasons. They fear going to the toilet will attract predators. When they eventually climb down to earth to go to the toilet, the sloths deposit up to two pounds of dung, around one-fifth of their total body weight. The rainy season makes all this hard work unnecessary. The rains mask the smell of their feces so the sloths defecate from high up in the trees.

*

The hoatzin, a Venezuelan bird, has a highly unusual stomach, similar to that of a cow. As a result its food ferments inside it producing a distinctive aroma, coincidentally much like fresh cow dung. The hoatzin's nickname is the stinkbird.

*

Penguins are among nature's super poopers. Chinstrap and Adelie penguins point their rear ends out of their nests, then fire their thick pink-and-white feces into the air with such force it lands up to 16 inches away. The technique helps the birds keep their feathers and nests clean. The long streak of penguin poo left in the snow soon disappears.

Few creatures can fire their feces with a force that can compete with the American silver-spotted skipper cater-pillar. It shoots its feces out of its rear at a speed of 4.3 feet per second and sometimes more, a force similar to that of a cannon. The feces can land as far as 60 inches away, a distance 30 times the insect's 1.6-inch body length. In human terms this would be the equivalent of 249 feet. Scientists believe the caterpillars do this not just because they are fastidious creatures but because dung is a magnet for predators.

Hippos use their tails to fling their feces over as wide an area as possible. The technique is designed to maxi-mize the amount of territory they mark out as their own. The male hippos rotate the tail quickly while they defe-cate sending their dung flying in all directions.

*

Farm animals are a major source of global warming. According to the United Nations, livestock such as cattle, buffalo, goats, sheep, camels, pigs, and horses are responsible for 30 percent of the methane emissions connected with human activities. Methane is the second-most important greenhouse gas after carbon dioxide.

Cows are thought to contribute 20 percent of the world's methane emissions. Dairy cows can belch 106 to 132 gallons of methane gas per day. That is 200 times more than a person. In a year they each emit 20 pounds of smog, forming gases known as volatile organic compounds (VOCs). That is more than a car or a light truck.

In New Zealand, 43 percent of its greenhouse gas emissions come from livestock. The burps of the country's 40 million sheep and 10 million cows produce 90 percent of its methane emissions.

Termites produce 4 percent of the world's methane. The gas brews inside the insect's hindgut and is released over its whole body.

*

If vultures feel threatened by predators they will often vomit violently in the direction of their attacker. They do not do so purely out of fear, however. By losing part of their body weight they will be able to take to the air and escape more easily. The foul-smelling vomit—among the most unpleasant aromas in the animal world—will also distract and possibly kill their attackers. Dogs have been known to die after coming into contact with vulture vomit.

Rats can't vomit. Other species have a reflex reaction that makes them throw up so as to reject toxic substances. Rats can't do this because their stomach and esophagus are separated by a barrier and they don't have the muscular strength to eject unwanted material back through it. Also, their brains can't coordinate their muscles to produce the necessary reaction. Instead, rats prevent themselves from swallowing toxic substances by having a highly developed sense of taste and smell. They also eat substances like clay when they feel sick. The clay binds the stomach and makes the nausea go away. Their inability to vomit is not the only by-product of their digestive handicap. They can't burp either.

Other animals that can't vomit include the rabbit, the house mouse, and the Japanese quail.

Under the Influence:
Animals That Get Drunk
and (Sometimes) Disorderly

Drug taking is common within the animal world. In West Africa, boars dig for the hallucinogenic roots of the iboga shrub, a drug that apparently sends them into a wild frenzy. Catnip appeals to cats because it contains the hallucinogen nepetalactone, which mimics a natural sex pheromone. Leopards and other big cats are also drawn to catnip and its Japanese equivalent, matatabi.

*

Among the animal world's most addictive drugs are hallucinogenic "magic" mushrooms. A leading ethologist once watched a jackal "spinning like a top" after eating some. Reindeer, too, are drawn to the mind-altering fungi. Their favorite is the red-capped *Amanita muscaria* mushroom, a strong psychedelic drug used by Siberian shamans. Such is the reindeer's craving for these mushrooms that they will get drunk on the urine of humans who have eaten them. Visitors to the Siberian tundra are warned not to urinate outdoors for fear of being charged by a mushroom-addicted reindeer.

Amazonian jaguars chew the bark of a hallucinogenic

vine. As well as giving them a high, the vine helps clear the jaguar's stomach of parasites.

*

Lemurs have their own version of ecstasy—a narcotic millipede.

The black lemurs on Madagascar eat the millipedes to extract a toxic chemical that acts like an insect repellant. But the act of eating millipedes sends the lemurs into an ecstatic trance. A scientist who studied this eating habit described the lemurs' eyelids drooping and their mouths frothing after eating the insects. They also "go all kind of sexy." The effect is short-lived, however, lasting for only a few minutes.

*

Farm animals freak out on weeds.

Cattle, sheep, and horses in the western United States and Mexico can get addicted to a plant nicknamed locoweed, or crazy weed. The weed is a tasty substitute for grass but is actually poisonous, containing an alkaloid called swainsonine which attacks the nervous system. As a result, an animal that gets hooked on locoweed starts behaving in an increasingly bizarre manner. First, they break away from the rest of their herd to become solitary eaters, then they start doing odd things like bumping into telephone poles and making exaggerated leaps into the air. They also develop a wobbly walk.

Too much of the locoweed can kill the animals. So farmers have developed a rehab program for addicted cows, sheep, and horses. Cold turkey consists mainly of eating so much salt with the weed it makes the animals violently sick.

*

In the mountains of Sikkim in northeast India, tired horses give themselves a gee-up by eating bitter tea leaves. Similarly, pack donkeys in Mexico graze on wild tobacco for the fillip it gives them.

*

Chimps can become just as addicted to smoking as humans. Ai Ai, a chimp at a Chinese zoo, started smoking cigarettes given to her by visitors shortly after her first male companion died in 1989 and started chain-smoking eight years later when her second companion died and her daughter was moved to another zoo. It was only after extensive therapy that she kicked the habit in 2005.

A dachshund lived to the ripe old age of 22—on ten cigarettes a day. When the dog was taken in after being abandoned he was found to like eating the tobacco and paper before spitting out the filter. Ordinarily nicotine is poisonous to dogs.

*

In the monkey world, drug taking is for the lower classes. In a study of a community of macaques, the more dominant, high-ranking monkeys tended to become less hooked on cocaine. Scientists think this may be because they get their kicks instead from being aggressive and domineering towards the subordinate monkeys.

*

Being exposed to marijuana in the womb makes young rats hyperactive and forgetful when they are born.

Goats can become addicted to caffeine, while ants can get hooked on nectar.

Rats can get hooked on testosterone.

Cocaine gives fruit flies a wild high. Scientists who exposed them to cocaine vapor watched as the flies spun around in circles and literally bounced off the walls.

*

Fermented fruit performs the same function for animals as alcohol does for humans.

When wasps gorge themselves on fermenting juices they can get so drunk they pass out.

Birds can get drunk too. In 2005, a large flock of cedar waxwings were treated at a wildlife center in South Carolina after they had all flown straight into the glass windows of an office block. The hundreds of waxwings were apparently intoxicated on holly berries.

African elephants are drawn to the smells of ripening marula fruits—which ferment into a 7 percent alcohol solution. For centuries many believed this makes elephants drunk and unsteady on their feet. Some scientists, however, doubt elephants could get drunk on the small amount they drink. They think the wobbliness may be caused by the marula tree's bark, which elephants also eat.

The bark is inhabited by the pupae of a beetle traditionally used to poison the tips of arrows.

*

Studies have shown hamsters can develop a taste for alcohol with a tolerance that is 40 times greater than humans' in proportion to their body weight. This is the equivalent of a human drinking a case of wine a day—with no visible effect.

As with humans, however, too much alcohol can make a hamster aggressive. It also produces a marked increase in the testosterone level of males. A hamster's drinking habit can, however, be suppressed by feeding it a Chinese herbal remedy, the extract of a kudzu root.

*

Pigeons get drunk on nuts.

The Seychelles blue pigeon feeds on Indian almonds. The nuts can become fermented, however. If the pigeons eat enough of the fermented almonds they will get so inebriated they won't be able to fly for several hours.

*

If only humans really could drink like fish. Scientists have learned that a key component of red wine, resveratrol, has the power to prolong life in a spectacular way. Flies and worms have been shown to live much longer and the results are even better in fish. A species of Zimbabwean fish that normally lives for just 9 weeks lived for between 30 percent and 60 percent longer when given high doses of resveratrol. At the age of 12 weeks, when they would normally be dead, many of the fish were active and had lively brains. However, humans thinking of taking in as much resveratrol as the fish would be advised to think again. To get the same amount of it into our systems would mean drinking the equivalent of 72 bottles of red wine a day.

*

Monkeys in India become drunk and disorderly. As many as 80 percent of monkeys in the province of Himachal Pradesh live in urban areas where they can get access to hard liquor. When they get drunk they jump on cars and bite children.

*

Elephants in Mongolia survive the freezing winters by drinking vodka. Members of the world-famous Moscow State Circus discovered that the spirit helped the performing elephants cope with temperatures that drop as low as -28°C (-18° Fahrenheit). A daily dose of two liters of vodka kept the cold at bay.

*

When it comes to boozing, rats divide themselves into four distinct groups. Scientists who introduced a group to alcohol saw the rats split into: teetotalers, social drinkers who imbibed only occasionally, a group that slowly increased their consumption to a high level then stayed there, and a few natural alcoholics who drank heavily from the very first day.

Stressed mice turn to the bottle for solace. Studies have shown that mice introduced to alcohol drink even more of it after they suffer upsetting events.

*

Caribbean monkeys get legless on rum.

Islanders on St. Kitts have learned to lure the island's vervet monkeys into their homes by leaving out coconut shells filled with the local sweetened liquor. The monkeys drink so much of the rum they end up in a stupor.

A scientific study found the monkeys have very different drinking habits. While around 1 in 7 did not drink at all, 1 in 20 monkeys were hardened boozers. These monkeys drank rum as fast as they could until they passed out. However, they seemed to suffer no hangovers. The next day they got up and did it all over again.

*

The elk is probably the worst drunk in the animal kingdom. In Sweden, in particular, elk gorge themselves on

aged apples, not realizing they have fermented. As a result they often end up in an aggressive, drunken stupor. Elk have been known to charge joggers. In 2005, a drunken party of elk surrounded an old people's home near Malmo and had to be removed by armed police.

PART THREE

THE BIRDS AND THE BEES: ANIMALS AND THEIR LOVE LIVES

Birds, bees, and of course, educated fleas do it. And such is the competition to reproduce, it can involve the briefest—not to mention the most frantic, violent, and even fatal—encounters.

Animal sex is not a purely random process, however. Many species go through long, complex—and occasionally romantic—courtships before choosing a partner with whom to share their precious genes. Just as in the human world, sex isn't always about reproduction. There are species that do it purely for kicks. And there are those who share the love that openly dares to tweet, whistle, and positively roar its name: homosexuality.

Looking for Mr. Right:
What Animals Want in Their
Ideal Partner

Most women find messy men unattractive and the female knot-tying weaverbird is no exception. She will refuse to mate with a male who has built a shoddy nest. If spurned, the male must take the nest apart and completely rebuild it in order to win the affections of the female.

*

Size definitely matters for females of certain fish species. Studies have shown that 8 out of 10 female mosquito fish prefer males who have large sex organs, or gonopodium. While this is good news for well-endowed male mosquito fish, there is a downside. Their size also makes them a favorite target for predators.

*

Female songbirds prefer males with big repertoires. Some female birds, like the great reed warbler, mate with males who have the widest range of tunes. Scientists believe this is because the size of a bird's repertoire is linked to the size of its spleen, which is in turn connected to the quality of its immune system. Studies have shown the offspring of warblers with big songbooks tend to survive longer.

*

Female frigate birds fall for the most inflated males.

As part of the courting process, males inflate throat pouches until they are the size of a balloon. Those with the biggest, reddest, and shiniest balloons attract the most female partners. Males have to be on their guard, however. The frigate bird is also equipped with a sharp bill and in an effort to steal their partner, other males may try to pop their rivals' balloons.

*

Female tamarin monkeys are attracted to good fathers so the males of the species pretend to be "new men." The monkeys carry children around with them; it is thought to show potential partners their parenting prowess.

*

Female deer are drawn to males with the best antlers.

To grow antlers, males need an excess of nutrients coursing through their bodies. So a male that eats on the run, feeding himself on the minimum he needs to survive, will not be able to grow antlers. On the other hand, a male with a large, treelike set of antlers exudes physical strength and well-being, because in order to grow them he must have had access to all the food he could eat. It also demonstrates that he has been able to fend off predators. Little wonder then that females are inexorably drawn to these magnificent-looking males.

*

The sexiest parrots have fluorescent feathers. Both males and females are attracted to those who have the brightly colored plumage, which glows by absorbing ultraviolet light. Humans can't see the effect normally, but scientists realized it existed when they noticed some dead parrots gave off an eerie glow when placed under a fluorescent light.

*

Female cockroaches like males with strong scents. They do, however, get less fussy as they get older and tend to follow the example of male cockroaches, who spend their lives mating with any female that has a pulse.

*

All that glitters is gold, as far as female butterflies are concerned at least. Female butterflies are attracted to males with a twinkle in their eyes. The sparkle is created by the ultraviolet reflection in the pupils of the butterfly's eyes. Females also draw partners to them by "flashing" light at them. The butterflies use the iridescent scales on their wings to produce a flash of brilliant blue color.

Fish also like a little bit of bling, it seems. Male stickle-backs build nests during the spring in the hope of attracting females to mate. A study discovered that when the fish decorated their nests with pieces of tin foil, the women flocked to join them in their gaudy new homes.

*

Male goby fish prefer females with red bellies.

*

Male giraffes have a novel technique for testing whether a female is ovulating. The male will hit the female's rear with his head to make her urinate. He then licks up a sample of the urine and, rather like a wine connoisseur testing a vintage red, finds out if she is ready to be impregnated.

*

Female voles prefer males who eat well. The voles are extremely picky and sniff out several potential partners before choosing one. Scientists have discovered that they tend to go for men who have eaten meals high in protein.

*

When looking for a mate, female impalas and wildebeests go for males with the best quality real estate.

Those with territorial control over good grazing land with tree cover and, even better, water supplies, are the most eligible bachelors. Those who rule over barren land are the least likely to get a mate. Predictably, this means male impala and wildebeest compete fiercely for control of the most desirable locations.

*

Female swallows prefer males who have long, symmetrical tails. Stunted and lopsided tails are a turnoff because they indicate bad genes.

*

Female gray partridges aren't impressed by macho males who fight all the time. They prefer men who watch out for them.

*

Female Mediterranean blenny fish set males to a test to see if they will be good fathers. The females leave the males to look after a trial collection of eggs for up to two days. If the eggs are safe when they return, the females will mate with the males.

*

The ideal man for a female peacock is the one with the most eyes, or oceli, within his spectacularly plumed tail. In a similar vein, female butterflies choose mates with big eyespots on their dorsal wings.

*

The pickiest creature in the animal kingdom may well be the female Californian fiddler crab. A study of a community of the crabs found that they inspected an average of 23 male crabs' burrows before opting for a mate. One unattached female inspected 106 before finding an acceptable mate.

*

Competition for the best males is tough among the topi antelopes of the Serengeti in Africa, so females will go to almost any lengths to get their man. They will engage in ferocious fighting with each other to claim the right male, but even if this is unsuccessful they will not give up. Some females will let her rival think she has prevailed, then charge into her once more the moment she starts mating.

*

Female horseshoe bats from different generations often mate with the same male. So a grandmother may procreate with the same male as her granddaughter. Scientists at Queen Mary, University of London, believe this is the bats' genetically hardwired way of safeguarding the colony's future, but it also creates a great deal of confusion. In several cases genetic tests showed that a female bat and her maternal half aunt also were half sisters on their father's side.

*

The crested auklet, an Alaskan seabird, has a very particular taste when it comes to sexual partners. It sniffs out members of the opposite sex that smell of tangerines. Scientists haven't yet explained why.

The Art of Seduction:
How Animals Impress the Opposite Sex

Male canaries can drive females wild with their singing. The birds can produce a spectacular, rapid-fire trilling, in which they vibrate notes 16 times per second. Such is the power of the canary's virtuoso voice, females who hear it immediately adopt a posture that signals they are ready for sex.

*

Humans aren't the only ones who show off their muscles to attract the opposite sex. Male sagebrush lizards do exercises as part of a complex system of body language the reptiles use to communicate with each other. To get the attention of prospective partners they do push-ups.

*

Giant pandas mark trees with scents to attract members of the opposite sex. Females urinate to leave a mark near the ground, while males pee or wipe their anal glands on the trunk. To show how fit and virile they are, the males compete to place these secretions as high as possible. To do this they adopt four main positions. The three most straightforward are a squat, a reverse wipe, and a leg-cock. To mark the tree as high as possible they adopt a more complicated, fourth position, a handstand.

*

The most elaborate courtship displays are those of the bowerbird.

These resourceful birds have unusually large brains, and the males of the species build complex structures—bowers—to impress their females. Some bowerbirds use twigs and shiny objects like shells and beetles to decorate the large, shed-like constructions. Others fill their nests with objects that are exclusively blue in order to attract females. Bowerbirds have been known to steal blue pens, bits of jewelry, and beads to make their homes seem more attractive to the opposite sex. Some psychologists argue their skills are worthy of comparison with human art.

*

Male fish build sand castles to impress the girls. Chichlid fish build these constructions, also known as bowers, not only to demonstrate their construction skills, but also the height of the bowers gives females a clear idea about the males' health. The bigger the castle, the better the genes are likely to be.

*

The appeal of a handsome sailor extends into the fish world. Female salmon prefer males who have traveled to sea and come home bigger, tougher, and wiser for the experience.

*

Male guppy fish know the way to a female's heart lies through her stomach. So they simply pretend to be her favorite food. The females particularly love bright orange fruits, so males have developed large orange spots on their stomach. The mere sight of the bright orange circles drives the female fish wild.

*

The male stickleback performs one of the marine world's most complex—and colorful—mating rituals.

When the spawning season arrives the tiny fish change color, with their undersides turning from their normal gray-green to a bright red. The male sticklebacks also leave their community to set up homes of their own, burrowing into the seabed and building pits that are filled with plant material and glued together with sticky fluid from their kidneys.

The completion of their nests is signaled by another change in color: this time the upper body turns a bluish white, which acts as a magnet for females.

It is after the nests are built that the males start doing the distinctive "zigzag" dance, in which they dart back and forth and rub their spines against females. If a female accepts the rubbing a male steers her to his newly built nest by turning on his side and pointing to it with his head. Once the female has laid her eggs in the nest, the stickle-back will fertilize and guard them diligently. Having gone to all this trouble to produce children, it is perhaps no surprise that the stickleback is a diligent dad as well. If a hatchling strays too far from home, the stickleback will swallow it up and spit it back into the nest.

*

Fireflies fall for each other under the insect equivalent of disco lights. The insects' abdomens contain a lantern fueled by a gas—nitric oxide. Males start the courting process by using their glowing stomachs to send out a well-choreographed series of flashes. Females respond with their own light shows. If they like what they see, the fireworks begin.

*

Male sailfin fish show off their sexual prowess by helping an all-female species, the Amazon molly, to fertilize their eggs. Because of the mollies' complex reproduction process, the sailfin isn't able to pass on its genes. But biologists have discovered the sailfin isn't wasting its time. Female sailfin fish who see their males involved with the other species find them attractive.

*

The North American bull elk mixes up his own version of a love drug.

To attract females, the elk engages in a complex, highly macho display. Among other things, he will ram tree trunks with his horns, ripping the bark off the tree. But his main technique for wooing female elk is to let out a deep, resonant bugling sound. As he does this he simultaneously sprays urine over his chest, neck, and stomach. The elk then digs a hole with his hooves and antlers, sprays yet more urine over himself until he is caked in a pungent smelling mud.

The aroma of the elk's eau de cologne is so powerful, females are soon wandering over, their heads bowed submissively, ready for mating.

*

Bats also smear themselves in their version of eau de cologne to attract females.

The greater sac-winged bat is so named because of the perfume-carrying sacs it has on its wings. The male of the species makes the perfume himself, mixing urine with a glandular secretion he obtains by rubbing his throat against his penis. He then inserts it into his wing sacs, heads off into the air, and hovers over females, wafting the scent over them. Female bats find the heady smell irresistible.

*

Female lobsters use a love drug to conquer their males. If a female wants to mate she squirts urine with a strong trace of sexual pheromones into the male's shelter. This calms the aggressive male down and makes him swoon. The female will also do a dance to entice him even more. By the time she enters the male's lair for sex, he is almost in a trance. The mating ritual ends with the female undressing. She can only mate after shedding her shell, and once she feels safe in the company of the alpha male she does so.

*

Snakes indulge in heavy petting. To get a female in the mood for love, a male snake will run his tongue along her

back and rub his chin against her body. He may also nuz-
zle up to her head or wrap his body around hers, then set
off a stream of muscle contractions that ripple against
her body. If he is successful the female will straighten her
body signaling her willingness to mate.

*

Rats get turned on by marijuana.

*

Earthworms are aroused by low doses of radiation.

*

Prairie voles become more interested in sex when the
long summer evenings set in. By contrast, cold winter
nights are a turnoff.

*

Female wood mice know there is a shortage of fertile
females willing to have sex with males, so they demand a
price for mating. The males must spend some time
grooming them first.

*

Penguins go in for prostitution. Female Adelie penguins willingly have sex with males in return for material to improve their nests.

*

Male southern right whales may be the best-behaved suitors in the animal world. They have to be.

Manners are an intrinsic part of the whales' community and it is no different when it comes to mating time. A female will mate with up to seven males. She will only do so, however, if they form an orderly queue.

*

As members of a species where males outnumber females by 10 to 1 during the breeding season, cuttlefish have to be especially cunning to mate successfully.

Small cuttlefish in particular adopt two main tactics. In the first they pick hidden corners of the seafloor where they signal to the available females. While the bigger cuttlefish engage in vicious fighting over mating rights, the small cuttlefish conduct secret rendezvous.

Their other trick is to change their body shape and skin patterns so that they look like females. This way they can sail past the bigger, more aggressive cuttlefish who guard their harem of females. Once they are in the clear, they change their markings back and start mating immediately.

*

What they lack in fitness, mature Japanese male crabs more than make up for in cunning. While young males chase females around above ground, the elderly sandbubbler crabs dig burrows in the mud. The more mature crabs know the females will come to the burrows to lay her eggs. When they do the old-timers ambush the females and mate with them again, this time in the knowledge that the last male to mate is usually guaranteed to be the father of her offspring. While the tactic is rather underhanded, at least it ends with a gentlemanly act. The old male gives the female his home so that she can raise her clutch of eggs there.

*

S is for sex, at least as far as guppy fish are concerned. To signal their readiness for mating, males of the fish species form their bodies into what is technically known as a sigmoid posture. Put simply, they form themselves into the letter S.

*

Bottle-nosed dolphins go through a highly energetic courtship ritual.

The male and female dolphin exchange vocal calls, then "kiss" by mouthing each other. They then move on to rub each other's genitalia and bodies, stroke each other's flippers, then engage in a lively game of chase. Finally, they display their affection for each other by butting heads.

*

Male midshipman fish have very different attitudes to courting. The males of the species divide themselves into two distinct types. The first take longer to mature, develop a strong vocal system, and learn to build good nests. The second put all their energy into becoming sexually mature and growing gonads that make up around 10 percent of their body weight. They also don't bother with a permanent home. When it comes to mating time, the difference in the two becomes even more marked. The nest builders try to subtly woo their females with melodic humming. The more macho fish don't bother with courting. They simply invade the first available nest and mate with the first females they can catch.

*

Male turtles have very different techniques for wooing females. Females are often disinterested in having sex and will move away if approached by an amorous male. The more romantic turtles persuade females to stay by titillating them with their claws. A male turtle will drum them on her closed eyes dozens of times in an effort to get her to consent. If he senses her compliance he rushes to the rear to take advantage.

This doesn't always work, however, so other males simply render their female partners immobile by biting their legs or shells. They then force themselves on the females to mate.

*

A species of North American snake has one of the most devious techniques for cornering all available females. By giving off a female chemical through their skins, male Canadian red-sided garter snakes can fool other males into having sex with them. Scientists believe they do this so as to drain all their rival males' energy. The transvestite males are then free to have sex with all the real females as much as they like.

The Mating Game:
Sex in the Animal Kingdom

Animals have wildly varying sex lives. When she is in heat, a lioness craves sex every half hour nonstop for five days and nights. The amazingly promiscuous female chimpanzee has been known to have sex with eight different males in fifteen minutes. At the other end of the scale some penguins only have sex twice a year. (This may have a lot to do with the sheer awkwardness of penguin sex, and the not-unrelated fact that homosexuality in penguins is common.) Even the penguin is promiscuous in comparison to the ultimate monogamous life form, the snail. Some breeds of snail only have sex once in their entire lifetime.

*

Humans, dolphins, and possibly dogs are the only species that have sex for pleasure, although the female pig must surely derive some satisfaction from her love life. Her orgasm lasts 30 minutes.

Buffalo sex takes five seconds.

Stick insect sex, on the other hand, can go on for several months. The smaller male attaches himself to the back of the female allowing her to get on with her life as he impregnates her. Biologists believe the male's possessiveness is a way of keeping other males at bay and ensuring the female's eggs will only be fertilized by his sperm.

*

Bonobos, or pygmy chimpanzees, are the only animals that use their tongues while kissing.

Tigers and lions will mate with each other. If the father is a tiger the child is called a tigon; if it is a lion, the cub is a liger.

*

The rooster is the Casanova of the farmyard. The lusty male copulates with hens for between ten minutes and an hour. Even so, if another mate presents herself immediately afterwards, he is usually able to oblige. This is because roosters have the ability to keep supplies of sperm in reserve.

*

The marine flatworm has perhaps the most bizarre form of sex. Scientists have called it "penis fencing." Flatworms are hermaphrodites with two sharp-ended penises. The mating ritual consists of two of them vying to pierce each other's skin with their penises. The first to land a successful blow earns the right to be the male and transfer his sperm. The "loser" has to take on the onerous task of letting the eggs develop inside her.

*

Only 1 in 20 cockroach matings is successful. Male cockroaches impregnate females via a spermatophore, a capsule packed with sperm. But the female often eats it because it is so rich in protein.

*

An insect called the springtail has one of the most elaborate, and indeed beautiful, mating rituals. The male produces a number of sperm-filled spermatophores and places them in a tightly packed circle around the female. He then does an energetic courtship dance designed to draw her out of the circle. When the female falls for the male's hypnotic dancing his cunning plan goes into action. The positioning of the parcels of sperm is such that one of them is almost certain to pass into her genital opening. Fertilization follows.

The mating ritual of the Caribbean reef squid is slightly less elegant. The male often lays a packet of sperm on the female's head.

*

Sex can often be a frantic affair. New Mexican spadefoot toads live in one of the world's hottest places and face temperatures of up to 48°C (118°F). For this reason they spend ten months of the year living underground. When they emerge in the rainy season their sexual urges are at fever pitch. They spend their brief time above ground conducting a frantic orgy. By the time they go back underground, most females will have laid 1,000 eggs.

*

The insect with the least romantic life may be the sand wasp. The male and the female of the species hatch from holes deep in the ground. They do so at different times, with the male emerging first. He quickly gets to sexual maturity and is soon frustrated by the fact that there are far more males than females. As a result, when a newly matured female sand wasp emerges from the earth, she is immediately pounced on by up to a dozen males. She remains buried underneath a flailing pile of fighting males until one emerges victorious and forces himself upon her.

Male garter snakes have an equally unchivalrous attitude to the opposite sex. The snakes hibernate in underground caverns during the winter but emerge in the summer when the temperature reaches the right level. The males always emerge first, sliding out in a mass, then waiting at the entrance to the cavern. The females come out one at a time soon afterwards. The instant they do so they are jumped by as many as 100 potential partners who wrap them up in a writhing ball. Within fifteen minutes the females' oviducts are full of sperm.

*

Romance isn't entirely dead in the animal world, however. Smitten whales behave like lovesick teenagers. When a male and female southern right whale get together to mate they caress, then roll around and embrace, locking their flippers as they go. They then lie side by side, shooting out water through their blowholes. They end their romantic ritual by diving out of the water in perfect synch.

Animal Parts:
Some Curious Things About
Sexual Organs

Many species have two penises. Male sharks, for instance, have two rolled-up pelvic fins. Snakes, lizards, and some crustaceans are similarly blessed. Male lizards who have the choice of using one of two penises when having sex tend to alternate between the two. Scientists have concluded they use the one with the best supply of sperm.

Spiders too have a pair of penises, in their case customized as parts of their mouths.

*

The earwig too has a second organ, in its case as a precaution against the other being damaged during sex. The risk is high because earwig penises can be longer than the insect's 1-centimeter (less than half-an-inch) body and so fragile that they can easily be snapped off during the coupling process.

The male red-billed buffalo weaver also has a false penis. The organ is a sexual aid to stimulate the highly promiscuous female of the species.

*

A lake-dwelling duck from Argentina has one of the more remarkable penises. The duck is only about 16 inches long, but its penis, when fully extended, measures 17 inches long. The base of the penis is covered with spines while the top is soft like a brush. Biologists believe the brush cleans out old sperm from the female's oviduct while the spines help the duck hold himself in place. When it is not required, the corkscrew-shaped organ retracts itself neatly into the bird's abdomen.

*

The southern right whale has a penis roughly 8 feet long, the biggest relative to its body size of any whale. Its testicles are its most impressive asset, however. They weigh over 2,204 pounds and are believed to be the biggest in the entire animal world. Marine biologists believe the right whale carries this much sperm so that, when its time comes to mate, the sheer force of the semen unleashed will wash out and replace any residual sperm from previous matings.

*

Cobweb spiders are too well endowed. To mate with their much bigger females, the male spiders have two giant sex organs called pedipalps. The organs are so big they account for 20 percent of the spiders' total weight and slow them down. By the time they reach adulthood the spiders have had enough of hauling these monsters around so they amputate one.

*

Pigs have corkscrew penises. They ejaculate a pint of semen each time they have sex.

*

Insects have the most complicated sexual organs.

The genitals of the European rabbit flea look more

like the inside of a clock than a body part. They have what look like springs, levers, hooks, and barbs attached to them. The cockroach has a curious collection of parts that look like a Swiss army knife. Some dragonflies have barbed whips at the head of their penis.

*

Who's been sleeping with my bedbug? The male bedbug is able to answer that question thanks to an "intelligent" penis, equipped with hairs that can detect whether a female has mated with someone else. Why female bedbugs would want to be promiscuous is another question altogether given the rather violent nature of bedbug sex. Males have needlelike penises which they use by stabbing the females in the stomach.

*

All male birds used to have penises. Now only 3 percent do. Among the minority are swans.

*

The fruit fly produces sperm that is almost 20 times as long as its body length. This is the equivalent of a human producing sperm more than 100 feet long.

Dangerous Liaisons:
How Sex (or the Lack of It) Can Kill

Male praying mantids take their life in their own hands when they have sex.

In many species of the insect, courtship doesn't exist. Instead females expect males to jump on them and copulate without even asking for permission. But there is a condition attached to this. Males should perform this maneuver in the correct way—creeping up from behind, then leaping on top of the female to grip her body.

If a male doesn't do this, the female may claim a terrible price: she will bite off his head.

In some species of mantids, there is no way a male can survive sex. The female will eat his head, then the rest of his body, while he continues to mate with her. Research suggests she does this for a very good reason. By disconnecting his brain from his body, the female neutralizes nerves in the male's head that inhibit him during mating. Once he is headless the male loses all these inhibitions and copulates repeatedly until the female has had enough.

*

Some males do all they can to ensure they end up as their partner's supper.

During sex, the male Australian redback spider, a close relative of the black widow spider, deliberately positions his abdomen over the jaws of the much bigger female, as if to say "eat me." The female usually obliges, although she doesn't kill him outright. Instead the male is able to copulate again by repositioning himself. The female will continue eating the male until she has finished having sex. She will then wrap the male up in a spun silk version of a "doggy bag" and finish the meal a little later.

Scientists think male redback spiders commit sexual suicide like this for three reasons. Firstly, spiders that are cannibalized by their partner have sex for longer times and therefore fertilize twice as many eggs. Also, females are more likely to reject other males if they have consumed a male partner. This gives the suicidal male a much better chance of fathering the female's children. Finally, the average life span of a male is only a few months compared to the two years a female can expect to live. He is unlikely to mate again in any case.

*

The insect world has plenty of man-eaters but few as mercenary as the female of one species of firefly. She uses her feminine wiles to lure a male, then eats him alive. This apparently has nothing to do with sex or dominance. The male produces a natural biochemical defense against the firefly's main predator, spiders. The female doesn't have this anti-spider serum. By eating a male whole the female gives herself a healthy immunizing dose of it.

*

Female funnel-web spiders tend to eat their males after sex, but some males have developed a clever way of avoiding this fate. They produce a dose of knockout gas that leaves females limp but still able to have sex.

*

Philandering fruit flies love fast and die young. The stress and physical effort of courting females reduces the life span of males.

*

The strain of being a successful stud can be tough.

Male elephant seals are among the most macho animals when it comes to sex. The giant, four-ton creatures fight a brutal battle for dominance at their breeding grounds. In smaller breeding communities, or rookeries, only the alpha seal will be allowed to mate, so contenders butt chests, tear at each other's face and skin with their teeth before one male emerges victorious. It's a questionable honor, however. An alpha seal may have a harem of up to fifty females that he has to mate with. The other males are so competitive that even after the alpha seal has won top spot he faces a constant threat from seals ready to usurp his position. As a result he doesn't eat for 100 days and suffers huge amounts of stress. The strain is so heavy that a male elephant seal's reign as the master of his harem is short-lived. While a tiny minority can stay on top for three mating seasons, many die in the 12 months following their tenure as the rookery stud.

*

Males in most species are obsessed with sex, but few creatures are so fixated on it as the moth. A sex-crazed moth is so obsessed with finding females that when it smells a potential partner it even loses its hearing, leaving it deaf to the sound of approaching predators like bats. This suicidal libido may well have something to do with the moth's life span. It only lives a fortnight.

*

Male mealworm beetles want to go out with a bang—literally. A study showed that dying beetles shut down their immune systems and concentrate all their energies on producing sex pheromones to attract females one last time.

The male honeybee also goes out with a bang. When he ejaculates he explodes. While the rest of his body is obliterated, his genitals remain inside the female, however. They remain there to prevent her from mating again, acting as a sort of insect chastity belt.

*

Female dung flies shake so violently when a male mounts them for the first time they become a blur. It is, perhaps, little wonder they are such nervous virgins. During sex the male dung fly's penis can damage her reproductive tract so badly she can't have sex with other flies.

*

Sex is also a fatal business for male quolls, members of a family of ferret-like marsupials. They die after just one mating season.

*

The mating process is an exhausting one, especially for the Pacific salmon. The fish travels thousands of miles to reproduce. As if this is not arduous enough, during the journey the females' hormones disintegrate their stomachs so that they have room to bear children. The trials don't end when they reach the breeding grounds. Males fight furiously for the right to mate, and the females scrap over which of them gets the best locations to give birth. Little wonder then that by the time the mass breeding has taken place and the salmon have produced the millions of fertilized eggs, the fish have no energy left whatsoever. They all die.

*

Just as in the human world, sex can carry health risks for animals, too. More than two hundred sexually transmitted diseases have been discovered in species from primates to insects.

Chlamydia and candida are sexually transmitted between birds. Chlamydia is also common among koala bears, and can lead to other illnesses, including pneumonia, arthritis, and infertility. Animals have their own versions of AIDS too, immune-deficiency viruses that can kill. Apes can get the simian version, SIV; lions can contract the feline strain, FIV. Insects like ladybugs can die from an AIDS-like virus transmitted by parasitic mites.

*

Few animals get as worked up about sex as elephants. When they are ready to mate, males enter a highly agitated state called musth.

It cannot be a coincidence that musth is derived from a Persian word meaning "drunk." While they are in this state the amount of testosterone in the male rises to 50 or even 60 times its normal level. They secrete a pungent mucus from a basketball-sized gland on the side of their cheek, pass as much as 317 quarts of urine daily, and become generally cranky and aggressive. The elephant can remain in this highly agitated state for anywhere from one week to four months. (Their frustration is not helped by the fact that females are in estrus for a mere 48 hours every four months. The opposite sex can also detect a male's quality as a breeding partner from his secretions and will reject those that aren't up to scratch.) During this time the frustration of not being able to mate can drive a male elephant close to death. They can lose weight and get terrible headaches.

*

The high level of testosterone coursing through the male ostrich's system at mating time turns the birds bright red. The ostrich's face, thighs, and long neck become scarlet. The more frustrated the males, the redder they all get.

*

A female ferret can stay in heat for 160 days and may die from anemia if it does not find a mate in this time.

Good Breeding:
How Creatures Practice Birth Control

Crayfish can clone themselves. The female of the marmokrebs crayfish can lay eggs despite having had no contact with any males. Her unfertilized eggs are then able to mature on their own, a process known as parthenogenesis. The African cockroach can clone itself using a similar process.

*

Snakes can have "virgin births." Several species, including some rattlesnakes, have been found to reproduce despite never having come into contact with a male. Scientists are unclear on how they do this.

*

Promiscuous creatures like the female cricket take precautions so as to avoid mating with the same male over again. The crickets usually mate with at least two different males each night, so they mark each partner with a scent that they use to make sure they don't repeat the encounter.

*

You could call it gull power. Female kittiwake gulls are so demanding about the quality of the sperm they use to reproduce they take care about the males they choose. Male gulls, like many male birds, store sperm for long periods of time before fertilizing their eggs. But as they wait to start the reproductive process they eject existing deposits of sperm so that it can be replaced by a fresher supply. Scientists studying the birds found the gulls' picky behavior makes sense. Kittiwakes who made use of older, stale sperm laid more eggs that failed to hatch, and the birds that did hatch successfully weren't as healthy.

*

Some mothers choose different fathers for producing sons and daughters. Female lizards, for instance, use sperm from bigger males to produce sons while they go for sperm from smaller males to produce females.

*

Many animals have their own sperm banks, designed to allow them to wait weeks, months, or even years before fertilizing their eggs. The Javan wart snake can store sperm for seven years, while other snakes and turtles can save it for four to five years. Turkeys are able to save sperm longer than any other bird. They have held on to it for 117 days. In comparison, sheep and pigs can hold sperm for just two days.

*

Males practice birth control, too. African millipedes have a cunning technique for guaranteeing they successfully fertilize female eggs. They scoop out the sperm from previous mates before inserting their own.

*

Weaker male iguanas save themselves for their partners. Aware they might be removed from their mates during sex by bigger iguanas, the smaller lizards ejaculate in advance then store the semen for later use.

*

Some male fruit flies have a crafty technique for ensuring their female partners remain faithful. Their semen contains a protein that keeps their sperm stuck inside, thus the female produces more eggs to lay. Female fruit flies can move on to other males within two days of mating, but the sticky sperm ensures that they shun other males for ten days.

*

The oceans are full of transsexual fish that change sex when the situation requires it.

Blue-headed wrasse, for example, live in groups where a larger male fish controls a harem of smaller females. If the male leaves the group, the largest of the females in the harem steps into his place. She will change herself into a male accordingly.

The reverse of this occurs in clownfish. They live in monogamous pairs with the female generally the bigger of the two. If the female leaves and her replacement is a female smaller than the male, the male and female switch roles so that they can produce the largest number of eggs possible.

Other gender-bending species, such as the Japanese goby, switch from male to female—and back again—as many as ten times in their lifetimes. These hermaphroditic fish are born with both testes and ovaries, so they can produce either eggs or sperm. Perhaps the most practical transsexual in the sea, however, is a species of sea bass which keeps its options open and functions as both sexes all the time. The bass is capable of switching from sperm production to laying eggs within 30 seconds.

*

Some species are perfectly happy without sex in their lives. The asexual bdelloid rotifer, a tiny creature found living in damp moss, lays eggs that don't need to be fertilized to mature into a new life. Its method of reproduction seems to work well enough. The rotifer has existed—and therefore gone without sex—for 85 million years.

As Queer as Folk:
Homosexuality in Animals

The most exhaustive study of the subject found that homosexuality is common in many species. Among those animals found to have same-sex relations were lions and giraffes, whales and dolphins, hedgehogs and vampire bats. The study's eye-opening discoveries included the fact that lesbian gulls share a nest to rear chicks together, male manatees have homosexual orgies, and male ostriches court other males by doing a pirouette dance. As part of their gay mating ritual, male lions rub their heads and roll around together. In a similar vein same-sex whales and dolphins rub their flippers together. Male giraffes indulge in passionate necking. The study found that oral sex is common among homosexual animals. Hedgehogs perform mutual licking of each other's genitals while male orangutans perform fellatio.

*

Homosexual dolphins have some of the most novel forms of sexual behavior, including nasal sex, in which a penis is inserted in the blowhole, and sonic sex, in which the dolphin's genitals are stimulated by sonic pulses.

*

Gay farm animals are commonplace. Female cows often mount each other, but do so to signal to the bulls they are ready to reproduce.

*

The supposedly sex-mad ram can also disappoint the shepherd who has bought him to impregnate his ewes.

As many as 16 percent of, or 1 in 6 rams, don't mate with females during the breeding or "tupping" season. Six percent aren't interested in sex, 10 percent are homosexual.

*

If one study of the subject is correct, the cowboy lovers probably weren't the only homosexuals on Brokeback Mountain. According to a scientist who studied their behavior for twenty years, mountain rams in the American Rockies live in an essentially homosexual society.

*

Male western toads have a basic problem when it comes to females—they can't tell the difference between them and their own gender. The toads don't let this get in the way when it comes to the mating season, however. If they come across a potential mate, they grab it and attempt to have sex with it regardless. Homosexuality is, therefore, rife.

*

The octopus experiments with homosexuality for a different reason. Because of the low populations of the deep sea creature, an octopus is likely to have very few opportunities to mate during its lifetime. Marine biologists believe that, as a result, an octopus has to explore the sexual possibilities of every fellow octopus it meets, regardless of whether reproduction is going to be possible. Homosexual behavior has been observed both in captivity and in the wild.

*

Atlantic bottle-nosed dolphins also find it hard to find enough sexual partners, so in desperation they have been seen trying to mate with a variety of other creatures. Sharks, turtles, seals, eels, and even humans are among the species that have been the targets of their amorous affections. Unsurprisingly, homosexuality and masturbation are common in this species of dolphin, too.

*

Homosexuality has been observed in both genders of Japanese macaque monkeys, but is particularly common to the females. A study found that during the breeding season female monkeys averaged seven different partners, only half of which were male. This may have something to do with the fact that while the females they mounted stayed around afterwards to groom, rest, and forage, the males took off almost immediately after sex.

*

Humboldt penguins form particularly strong gay partnerships. Attempts by a German zoo to break up a group of
six homosexual penguins by introducing a group of
females failed miserably. The males simply became closer,
and when they sensed the females' interest in breeding
they pretended rocks they kept in their caves were actually eggs they were incubating. The females quickly lost
interest.

*

Ducks practice homosexual necrophilia. A mallard duck
was observed having sex with another male that had died
after flying into the glass façade of Rotterdam's Natuur-
museum. A curator who witnessed the gruesome act—
the first ever recorded—watched the live duck astride
the dead duck for seventy-five minutes. Unable to watch
any longer he separated the ducks and performed an
autopsy on the dead bird.

Till Death Do Us Part:
Fidelity and Infidelity in Animals

Fidelity, although rare, does exist in the animal world. Birds are more likely to remain faithful to a partner than are other animals. Around 9 out of 10 birds are believed to practice social monogamy, that is staying with the same partner. (This is compared to around 1 in 20 of mammal species, where only gibbons, jackals, and tamarins show high degrees of fidelity.) The most devoted birds are, unsurprisingly, lovebirds, who sit in pairs, constantly preening and petting each other throughout their "married" life. (They don't play the grieving widow or widower when their partner dies, however, and waste no time in finding a new love.) Other species that tend to stick to the same partner for life include the Bewick's swan and the waved albatross. Among the least faithful birds are house martins and greater flamingos, whose pairings all end in "divorce."

*

While songbirds have a reputation for monogamy, some species simply can't stop themselves from having extra-marital relations. In some cases, up to 75 percent of females cheat on their nest mates. For instance, around 40 percent of collared flycatchers have affairs. Most are tempted by males sporting large white spots on their fore-heads. These birds are irresistible to the female flycatchers because they tend to father plump chicks.

*

Infidelity can carry a high price. The dominant alpha male in a community of macaque monkeys has the right to mate with every female in the group. No other male is allowed to have sex with them. However, the alpha male tends to keep a harem of the most desirable females. Females rejected from his first team flirt with other males, tempting them to risk quick sexual encounters when the alpha male is distracted. Many are successful, but many are also discovered by the leader or exposed by spies within the community. The alpha male's revenge can be bloody and fatal.

*

Condors can't do love triangles. The giant birds of prey are naturally monogamous throughout their lives, a trait that is probably connected to the intense nature of child rearing. The male and female must spend two years care-fully guarding, incubating, and rearing the one egg the mother produces whenever she breeds.

A rare sighting of a male with two female partners revealed a trio of very confused birds. Each female had produced an egg with the male, but when left alone in the nest the mothers moved around in an agitated state as if they didn't know which one to protect. As a result at least one of the chicks died.

*

Henpecked male budgies have affairs behind their partners' backs—and for good reason. Given the choice of
mating with a female other than its partner, the male's
choice will depend largely on whether there is a chance its
partner will discover its transgression. The male's cau-
tion is understandable. Female budgies find it easy to
attract replacement males. The females also react to cheat-
ing males by delivering angry chirps and jabbing the males
with their sharp beaks.

*

The bird with the strictest attitude towards monogamy is
probably the black vulture. Any member of a black vulture group caught trying to have sex with a bird other
than its partner is immediately attacked by every other
vulture nearby.

*

Marmosets make particularly faithful fathers. The smell of
an ovulating female usually sends males' testosterone
levels soaring. If the males have had offspring with other
females, however, they resist the urge and stay true to their
partners.

*

Cockerels have a simple but highly effective technique for
keeping their hens faithful—they pretend to have regular
sex with them.

The birds have a harem of females and are highly pos-
sessive of them, with good cause because of their promiscuity. To keep them sweet, cockerels regularly mount
their hens but hold back from releasing any semen.

The duped hens would feel even worse if they knew the double standards their males were applying. If a cockerel encounters a hen he doesn't know he will almost certainly be unfaithful. Not only will he have proper sex, he will willingly give her all the semen he has, too.

PART FOUR

FAMILY AFFAIRS:
THE TRIALS AND TRIBULATIONS
OF ANIMAL PARENTHOOD

Starting and raising a family is a testing, stressful business. If the emotional roller coaster of childbirth isn't grueling enough, there is the nerve-racking challenge of feeding, nursing, and nurturing the helpless newborn—several hundred of them in many cases.

Nature's mothers and fathers deal with all these things, as well as the constant threats from predators—not to mention siblings and stepparents—who want to kill or eat their offspring. And how do their kids thank them for it?

When the Stork Comes:
A Few Odd Facts About Animal
Reproduction

Female cheetahs don't ovulate if there are other females around. The cheetah is one of the most solitary of all animals, and scientists believe the presence of another female creates stress that disrupts the cat's hormone cycle.

*

Once female kangaroos reach puberty they can remain constantly pregnant and constantly producing milk until they die.

*

Giraffes give birth standing up. The fact they emerge so high off the ground doesn't cause a problem for their babies—they are at least six feet tall at birth. The young giraffe grows at the rate of an inch per day and doubles in height within a year.

*

The female pigeon cannot lay eggs if she is alone. In order for her ovaries to function, she must be able to see another pigeon. If no pigeon is available, her own reflection in a mirror will suffice.

*

Guppy fish like to keep up with their neighbors, especially when it comes to children. The more guppies a female sees in her neighborhood, the more offspring she produces.

*

Temperature is a crucial factor in determining the sex of a newborn animal. Whether an alligator is a male or female is often determined by the temperature of the nest where the egg is hatched. If it is between 90° and 93°F the baby will be male. If it is between 82° and 86°F it will be female. Many animals have developed an ability to judge temperature accurately. The iguana can measure the heat of the sand where it lays its eggs to within two degrees Fahrenheit. Females of some lizard species in the mountains of southeastern Australia uniquely use this method to choose the sex of their offspring. They control their own body temperature so as to produce male or female young, as required.

*

Darwin's frog, a rare breed from Chile, has a unique way of nurturing its young. When the female has laid the eggs the male takes over, first guarding them, then swallowing them whole. The eggs grow in his vocal pouch before hopping out of his mouth when they have developed fully.

*

The giant *Mola mola,* or ocean sunfish, can carry up to 300 million eggs in a single ovary, more than any other vertebrate.

*

The sea horse is unique—the only animal in which the male of the species gets pregnant. During sex the female positions a long tube called the ovipositor alongside the male pouch. The eggs then move along the tube into the pouch where the male fertilizes them. The "mother" plays a minimal role during pregnancy, popping in to check the pregnant father for ten minutes or so a day. When, between ten days and six weeks later, the embryos have fully developed the male sea horse will go through labor on his own, too. Nature's ultimate Mr. Mom will deliver his brood by pumping his tail up and down. Male sea horses can bear between a few dozen and a hundred babies, although one Caribbean male has been recorded as giving birth to a prodigious 1,500 sea-ponies.

*

Birds in the Northern Hemisphere lay more eggs than those in the southern half of the world. Researchers believe that since northern birds face tougher winters they know the survival rate of their young will be lower. Birds down south tend to put their own survival above that of their young.

*

Stress is bad for pregnant ewes and their offspring. Studies have shown mothers-to-be that endure anxious pregnancies produce equally uptight lambs. Lambs born to ewes with high levels of the stress hormone cortisol suffer from high blood pressure.

*

The smallest tortoise lays some of nature's biggest eggs, relative to its size. The tiny speckled padloper, which is only 2.75 inches long, produces an egg that is just over 1 inch, 40 percent of its body size. That's the equivalent of a five foot human mother producing a child two feet tall.

*

The kiwi lays the largest egg relative to its size. Kiwi eggs can weigh a quarter of the female's weight, the equivalent of a human mother giving birth to a 35-pound baby.

*

Female orca whales give birth, on average, once every ten years. Their offspring emerge tail first, weighing 400 pounds and measuring 8 feet long.

*

Chicken eggs are either white or brown. Of the four kinds of chicken, only Mediterranean chickens produce the white variety. European, Asian, and American chickens produce the brown type. The easiest way to detect which kind of egg a hen will produce is to look at the chicken's earlobes. Mediterranean chickens have white earlobes, the others have red ones.

*

Rats produce offspring at a prodigious rate. Female black rats, for instance, give birth to between four and ten babies after just three weeks of gestation. Given their promiscuity it is reckoned that within 18 months two rats could have more than a million descendants.

*

Animals can produce litters containing offspring by more than one father. A study of white-tailed deer in the United States revealed that twin fawns born to a mother had different sires. Intriguingly, the dads turned out to be from different generations, one a young buck and the other an older deer. Scientists think the older deer interrupted the younger one during mating, impregnating the female for a second time. Similar findings have been reported in squirrels.

*

The giant panda's status as one of the world's most endangered species is in part because of its inefficient breeding habits. Females can conceive only once a year and are receptive to a male for only three days annually. If a successful conception produces twins—which it does in 60 percent of cases—the mother will only care for one of her offspring. The other panda will be abandoned to die.

Newborn pandas are among the smallest mammal

babies, relative to the size of their mother. They can weigh as little as 4 to 6 ounces, lighter than an apple. They grow very slowly, taking up to four years to reach their full adult weight.

*

Gorillas experience menopause, too. Females can live to be more than 50, but they don't have babies after the age of 37. No other animal is known to lose the ability to reproduce in this way.

*

SOME ANIMAL GESTATION PERIODS (in days)

Ass: 365

Bear: 180–240

Cat: 52–69

Chicken: 22

Cow: 280

Deer: 197–300

Dog: 53–71

Duck: 21–35

Elephant: 510–730

Fox: 51–63

Goat: 136–160

Groundhog: 31–32

Guinea pig: 58–75

Hamster, golden: 15–17

Hippopotamus: 220–255

Horse: 329–345

Human: 253–303

Kangaroo: 32–39

Lion: 105–113

Monkey: 139–270
Mouse: 19–31
Parakeet (Budgerigar): 17–20
Pig: 101–130
Pigeon: 11–19
Rabbit: 30–35
Rat: 21
Sheep: 144–152
Squirrel: 44
Whale: 365–547
Wolf: 60–63

Maternal Instincts:
Nature's Best (and Worst) Mothers

A new mother blue whale produces up to 94 gallons of milk per day. She has to—she is in charge of a baby with a quite gargantuan appetite. A baby blue whale grows at a phenomenal rate, putting on more than 10 pounds an hour and 250 pounds each day. To keep pace with this the baby needs to feed up to fifty times a day and can drink 2.5 gallons at each feeding.

*

As all new parents know, looking after a newborn may require sleepless nights. But scientists have discovered that killer whales and bottle-nosed dolphins go an entire month without any sleep. They do this not only to avoid predators, but also to keep the newborn warm until it develops its first layers of insulating blubber. Surprisingly, it seems to have no ill effect on either the parents or their offspring. Both remain alert and on the move throughout this time.

*

Young dolphins suck up to their mothers for good reason. For the first three years of their lives, the calves swim with their mothers and have to somehow keep up. They manage this by positioning themselves in their mother's slipstream where they are literally sucked along.

*

Insect parents can't listen for the sound of their children crying out for food because the larvae can't make noise. So insects, like burrower bugs, keep their smell receptors open for chemical signals from their larvae. A study concluded that all parent bugs need is a whiff of distress and they know what the little ones want.

*

The tilapia mother has a highly effective technique for defending her young at times of danger. At the first sign of a threat the female fish opens her mouth and sucks her young up into an oral cavity where they remain until the coast is clear.

*

Rat mothers raise well-adjusted children. Rats brought up by attentive mothers grow up to be more adventurous. They are also less sensitive to stress.

*

Grouse give off a powerful scent that can be detected by predators. The scent disappears when it is incubating eggs, however, leaving it and its young relatively safe from attack.

*

Spotted hyenas are thought to be the only mammals that produce infants genetically programmed to attack and, if possible, kill their siblings.

*

Midwifery is rare in the animal world, but a few mammals help their fellow females give birth. Marmosets, elephants, and bottle-nosed dolphins have been observed helping each other out during labor. But the most remarkable sighting was that of a fruit-eating bat. A female Rodrigues bat from Mauritius was seen showing a novice mother the right position to give birth, then licking and grooming both her and the child through the labor. After the birth the "midwife" bat even led the baby bat to its mother's nipple for the first time.

Pregnant kangaroos and wallabies can keep embryos in suspended animation. If conditions aren't right and there is bad weather, sickness, or a shortage of food or space in her pouch, the mother releases a substance from her mammary gland that puts the embryo's development on hold in a state called diapause. She will only restart the growing process when the conditions are right.

*

Some penguin mothers practice tough love. Female chinstrap penguins raise their young in crèches and run away from their chicks when it's feeding time. Only those quick enough to catch up are fed. Scientists think the penguins do this to test which chicks are fit enough to be worthy of rearing.

*

Honeybees are doting parents. If there is a hint of a problem in the "nursery," they will change their normal routines to stay up all night with their larvae. They are thought to be one of the only insects to do this.

*

Spanish deer give their sons better quality milk. The Iberian red deer produce milk with higher levels of protein for male calves. Scientists think this is done because males can produce more offspring than females.

*

Kangaroos grow on trees.

A rare, tree-dwelling species of the marsupial lives in the rainforests of New Guinea and North Queensland in Australia. Mothers raise their young high off the ground where they are safe from earthbound predators.

*

European starlings create a healthy nursery for their children. The starlings decorate their homes with a collection of plants that include wild carrot greens, agrimony, yarrow, and fleabane. Scientists think they are effective in preventing bacteria and fungus growing inside the nest and can also stop lice, mites, and ticks from hatching. They stock up on the plants during breeding. The carrot greens, in particular, have also been shown to improve chicks' levels of hemoglobin.

*

Being born to a single mother needn't be a disadvantage; indeed, it is a distinct asset if you are a male finch. Male zebra finch chicks cared for by their mother alone get, on average, 25 percent more food than they would if their father were around. What's more, when the sons of single finch mothers grow up they are more attractive to the opposite sex. Females swoon at the bigger builds the extra food gives the fatherless finches.

*

Egret mothers breed three chicks knowing they are going to lose one.

The egret is only capable of raising two but has three as an insurance policy. When she is sure the two first born

are healthy and will survive she lets them kill the third
sibling.

*

Cockroaches get no parental care at all. Newly hatched
roaches are simply left to fend for themselves.

*

Beware sparrow second wives. Because a bigamous male
will tend to care for the nestlings he had with his first
partner rather than any future mates, the second wives
take drastic action and kill their rival sparrow's children.
Such female infanticide is very unusual in the bird world.

*

Bear-back riders. Sloth bears carry their young on their
backs. They are the only mammal, apart from the occasional human dad, known to do this.

Paternal Instincts:
Nature's Best (and Worst) Fathers

Some male partners have sympathetic pregnancies. Two species of Brazilian monkeys, tamarins and marmosets, both put on significant amounts of weight during their partners' pregnancies. Some marmosets gain as much as 20 percent in weight while their partners are pregnant. Both species are monogamous and unusually devoted partners, particularly tamarins. They take an active part in child rearing and carry their babies around more than the mother does. Scientists think the bulging waistlines help prepare the monkeys for the workload ahead.

Male monkeys from other species develop milk hormones during the last fortnight or so of their partners' pregnancies. In females, the hormone prolactin prepares the mammary glands to produce milk. In males, however, it is thought to prepare them for the stresses of parenthood. The more experienced the dad, the more of the hormone he produces.

*

The male emperor penguin faces as tough a parenting challenge as there is anywhere in the animal world. For two months he must protect a single egg, allowing it to incubate under his body in the face of the harsh Antarctic winter. Males bulk up in preparation for this job and weigh around 88 pounds when they start their epic egg watch. By the end they are half this size.

*

The Australian marsupial frog has a novel way of keeping a fatherly eye on his young. He lets his partner's tadpoles crawl along his back, then slide into a slot that leads to a pouch on his hip. The tadpoles remain there for a few weeks, feeding on leftover yolk from their former home in the egg, then jump out as matured frogs. Since this behavior was first spotted the frog has been awarded a new name, the hip-pocket frog.

*

The South American marmoset is one of the most involved fathers. He is on hand during birth to act as a midwife, grooming and licking the newborns as they emerge. He then feeds, grooms, and carries the young around during their first weeks of life. This hands-on attitude has much to do with the toll childbirth takes on the female marmoset. Children can weigh a quarter of her body weight, the equivalent of a 140-pound human giving birth to a 35-pound child. The females also tend to get pregnant again within a fortnight.

*

Male lions are ruthless when they join a pride that is unprotected by other males. They immediately kill all the cubs that are too small to elude them. The tactic ensures that the male's new partner gets back into season around eight months sooner than if she'd carried on nurturing her cubs. This allows the male to begin producing his own cubs as soon as possible.

*

Males from hot climates make worse dads. Evidence suggests male monkeys in the tropics are more likely to desert their mates once they have given birth. By contrast, male monkeys in cooler climes stay around and help with the child rearing. Anthropologists believe this may be linked to the lower survival rates in colder climates. Males there hang around to give their offspring a better chance of living.

*

The Japanese cardinal fish may be the animal world's worst dad. The males of the species are entrusted with caring for their broods. They do this by keeping their young safely in their mouths until they are mature enough to be released into the ocean. Unfortunately, the cardinal fish is not monogamous. If he sees a female that is more attractive than his current partner he will begin courting her. Not wanting to be seen as a male with "baggage," he eats his children before doing so.

Little Monsters:
Troublesome Children
and How Animals Cope with Them

Male budgerigars are soft touches as fathers. While budgie mothers feed their young according to a strict order and will not be manipulated into favoring one child over another, fathers are a different matter. When they feed the family they tend to give food to those who make the loudest and most persistent noise.

*

For pure drama at feeding time, few can match the pelican chick. To let their parents know they are hungry, young pelicans throw themselves at their parents' feet, thrashing around and even biting their mother, father, and siblings. If this doesn't work, they can literally throw a fit, going into convulsions in a final effort to persuade their parents to feed them.

*

Owls employ snakes as child minders. To keep their chicks safe, screech owls enlist the help of blind snakes which normally live underground. To keep the lodgers happy in the nests, owls feed the snakes on grubs. In return, while the mothers are away the snakes scare off any predators that might have ideas about stealing the chicks. The snakes clearly do a good job. One in 5 owls has snakes in its nest. Studies have shown these chicks grow up faster and are much more likely to survive than the offspring of the 4 in 5 owls who don't have a pet reptile.

*

Finding good child care is a problem in the animal world too. White-winged choughs solve the problem by kidnapping other birds to help with the raising of their young.

*

Spotted flycatchers carry on begging their parents for food long after they are ready to fend for themselves. Parents have to take drastic measures to get their youngsters to stand on their own two feet—they run away at mealtimes.

*

Rich parents are more likely to have stay-at-home sons, at least in the bird world. Studies revealed that the maturing male and female offspring of Californian bluebirds with good supplies of mistletoe berries behaved very differently when it was time to fly away from home. While the girls left home to make their own way in the world, the boys hung around to live off their parents' wealth.

*

Troubled childhoods give rats mental problems in adult life. Studies have shown suffering high levels of stress in their early life produces shrunken brains and loss of memory.

*

Young grizzly bears tend to make their homes close to their mothers.

*

Monkeys seek teenage kicks, too. Adolescent vervet monkeys take much greater risks than infants or older ones. They will even attempt to steal food in full view of potential predators.

*

Teenagers who are suddenly oblivious to anything their parents say aren't confined to the human world. Tadpoles go temporarily deaf just before they metamorphose into frogs.

A Death in the Family:
How Animals Cope with Loss

Divorce or the loss of a partner sends gerbils into a deep depression. The rodents form close, lifelong partnerships, and if they are separated from their partner they struggle to sleep properly and become socially withdrawn.

*

Sea lion mothers unfortunate enough to witness their babies being attacked and eaten by killer whales make a heartrending noise, a mixture of squeals and wails.

*

Dolphins have been observed trying to revive their dead offspring.

*

Monkeys can be overcome by grief. A chimpanzee was so consumed by the loss of its mother, it removed itself from its group, stopped eating, and eventually died.

Similarly, a study discovered that a dominant female baboon who lost her closest companion went into mourning afterwards. The dead baboon, who was killed by a lion, had been the queen baboon's grooming partner and the only member of the community with whom she fraternized. After her friend's death, the queen's levels of the stress hormone glucocorticoid shot up to levels that were much higher than those in the rest of the community. The queen also began allowing the lower-ranking members of the community to groom her, lowering her stress levels.

*

Elephants are particularly sensitive to death.

Mothers have been seen keeping a lengthy vigil over a stillborn child. The giants stay there for days with their heads and ears hung down in what looks to be an expression of utter despair. Young elephants can be so traumatized by witnessing their mothers' deaths that they have been observed waking up in the middle of the night screaming.

Elephants also pay their respects to the dead and may be drawn to graveyards.

Unlike most animals, who may ignore or even eat the body of a member of their own species, elephants become agitated by the sight of a fallen elephant. They also pay an unusual amount of attention to the bones and skulls of elephants that have been dead for many years.

Scientists think there may be truth in stories that ele-

phants make journeys to visit the last resting place of relatives. The idea that old elephants have "elephant graveyards," specific places they head off to die, however, is
probably false.

*

Birds appear to grieve, too. Greylag geese have been seen
seemingly wracked by the loss of their partner. The birds'
eyes seem to sink deeper into their sockets and their bodies sag with their heads hanging low.

*

No creature is better equipped to deal with a broken
heart than a zebra fish. It can regenerate missing or damaged heart muscle.

A MATTER OF LIFE AND DEATH: HOW THE FITTEST, STRONGEST, SMARTEST, AND DOWNRIGHT NASTIEST SURVIVE

We call it the law of the jungle, but nature's most basic principle is enforced just as cruelly on the ocean floor and the Arctic tundra. Only the strongest survive, and across the animal world, strength is measured in simple terms. Who can conduct the most effective form of warfare, whether it be conventional, chemical, or even psychological?

No Holds Barred:
How Animals Fight

Rats settle disputes by boxing. Two female spiny rats were filmed in the Amazon area of Peru punching, grabbing, shoving, and pushing each other for a period of ten minutes.

*

Male kangaroos box as a form of play. Young males stand up on their hind legs and spar like boxers in a gym. Their rules are more similar to those of Thai boxing than those of the Marquess of Queensberry. Their preferred form of defense is to kick each other.

Many kangaroos continue to box into their adulthood. As a result males develop heavily muscled forearms and broad chests. Some look so intimidating that they will win contests against smaller males simply by puffing out their chests and flexing their muscles like a prize fighter who has just won the world title.

*

Cockroaches wrestle to the death. Males begin their contests for dominance by squaring up to each other with their heads low and their bodies raised at the rear. They then charge at each other so as to butt each other with their heads. If one of the insects succeeds in getting his protruding pronotum (the dorsal area between his head and his body) under his opponent, he will flip him into the air so that he lands on his back. If not, the two will grapple with their legs locked together. During this phase of the fight they will bite each other and roll over and over. A victor will soon emerge. Even if he has survived physically, the loser will soon die from the stress of the fight.

*

Fruit flies Sumo wrestle. In scientifically observed fights, the insects adopted one of two styles: grappling each other with their forelimbs like tired boxers or shoving each other out of the arena like the overweight Japanese wrestlers.

*

Macaque monkeys are masters of fighting dirty.

If Japanese macaques lose a confrontation with another monkey, they take it out on one of the rival's weaker relatives. This generally dissuades their rival from attacking them again.

Stump-tailed macaque monkeys, on the other hand,

wait until their male rivals are at their most vulnerable. Working in gangs of up to nine monkeys, they wait until their victim is having sex, then jump him at the precise moment he is reaching an orgasm.

*

Know thine anemone. Sea anemones fight in armies, with individuals divided up into different classes of soldiers, scouts, and other ranks.

Anemones live in large colonies at the edge of the sea. When the tide is out, all is quiet. But when the tide is high one colony comes across another and madness ensues. First, scout anemones move in to find a suitable space to fight a battle. As they do this, warrior anemones prepare their weapons, pumping up special stinging tentacles. Meanwhile, another class of anemone continues to clone new anemones to join the army.

The battles are usually short and brutal, with the two warrior armies trading blows with their tentacles. A successful hit leaves a painful stinging cell glued to the victim's body. After roughly half an hour the fighting stops.

*

Wild stallions warm up for fights by squealing at each other. Scientists believe the ritual is a way of showing off lung capacity and therefore fitness. The stallions understand that the horse with the longest-lasting squeal is likely to be the best fighter. This may help explain why half of stallion fights end quickly with one horse running off before meaningful blows have been exchanged.

*

The robin's image as a symbol of peace and goodwill at Christmastime is undeserved. Despite its size, the little red-breasted bird is highly confrontational and frequently involved in fights over territory. Robins have also been observed harassing hedge sparrows for no obvious reason. Robins launch vicious attacks involving furious pecking of their opponents' heads, but this can backfire badly. Ornithologists believe 1 in 10 robins die from the fractured skulls they get when they end up losing a fight.

*

Much like football fans, fish get aggressive simply watching other fish competing with each other. Scientists believe the rise in testosterone levels prepares them in case they too are challenged and have to defend themselves. Unlike football fans, the testosterone levels don't fade at the final whistle. Tilapia fish remained in an agitated, aggressive state for six hours after watching other fish fight.

*

American lobsters can smell when they are going to lose a fight. Lobsters rely on smell to recognize fellow lobsters, and the highly competitive males in particular use it to identify other males with whom they have fought. If a male lobster does not recognize a scent, it will attack.

*

Many animals need to get their aggression out of their system—even if there isn't any obvious target.

Some pick a fight with themselves. Mongooses and chickens, for instance, attack their own tails while male white wagtails pick a fight with their own reflection. The birds have been observed making aggressive signs to their distorted reflections in car bumpers.

Perhaps the most desperate attempts to start a fight, however, are those staged by the yellowtail damselfish. It picks fights with its food.

Natural Born Killers:
Nature's Ultimate Hitmen

Sharks are mass murderers even before they are born.

A mother sand tiger shark produces hundreds of embryos at the same time. As they grow inside her womb, each embryo produces tiny razorlike teeth. During the pregnancy the embryonic sharks will attack and kill each other. After three or four months of battling, only a handful of dominant shark embryos will remain alive. These remaining sharks will then have a final struggle in which only one shark will survive. It will then emerge into the sea as a full-fledged killing machine.

Marine biologists have had nasty surprises when studying these shark embryos. At least one has received a painful bite from a shark embryo while examining the inside of its pregnant mother's womb.

*

Cookie-cutter sharks have a sneaky technique for trapping their prey. The cookie-cutters have a dark band under their jaws that looks like the outline of a much smaller fish. They also have light-emitting cells which make them glow, and when they swim near the water's surface the cells help them to blend in with the light from the sky above. The result of this is that a predator such as a tuna will not see the whole of the shark when it views it from underneath. Instead it will see what looks like a sitting target. It gets a rude awakening when it swims up for the kill. This is when the cookie-cutter lives up to its name, gouging out round, cookie-shaped chunks of flesh from its victims.

*

Japanese honeybees show no mercy when they catch a giant hornet in their nest. Hundreds of bees swarm around the destructive pest. They then roast it alive with their body heat.

*

Spiders are sophisticated hunters and can customize their webs according to the prey they are chasing. South American spiders have been seen building smaller, fine-meshed webs for flies then constructing much bigger, wider-meshed webs to catch termites.

*

Rattlesnakes rattle to charge themselves with static electricity. They then use the power to electrically sense good places to hide and catch prey.

*

Snakes squeeze the life out of their prey by constricting them. A python has been measured creating a force of more than 14 pounds per square inch, six times the strength of the firmest of human handshakes.

*

Puffins may be the bird world's greatest hunters. One species, the tufted puffin, can routinely emerge from the water with between five and twenty fish in their bills. In one recorded instance, a bird was seen with sixty-five fish in its mouth.

*

The killer whale, or orca, is one of nature's most ingenious predators, with a wide range of tricks for capturing its prey. Orcas have been known to beach themselves in order to catch sea lions, upend ice floes to tip seals and penguins into the sea, and slap their tails on the water's surface to wash birds off rocks into their path. Their most spectacular trick, however, is reserved for sharks. The orca kills its deep-sea rival by torpedoing up into the shark's stomach from underneath, causing it to explode.

*

Crocodiles don't leave leftovers after eating. Their digestive juices are so acidic they can break down skin and bone and even animal horns.

*

Some animals are dangerous even when they're technically dead.

Rattlesnakes, for instance, can still deliver a nasty bite after they have been shot or beaten to death. A study of the snake's ability to strike from beyond the grave cited one rattler that had been shot and decapitated then left for five minutes, until there were no more signs of movement. When the hunter picked up the snake's head it lunged at him and bit him. It did this not once but twice.

*

As if the South American giant tarantula isn't scary enough to look at, it also makes a terrifying hissing noise that sounds like Velcro being ripped off.

*

Horned frogs lure their prey by clever sleight of hand. The frogs camouflage themselves so that only one of their feet is visible. They then wriggle two of their toes so that they look like worms or insect larvae. Lizards, mice, birds, or frogs that are drawn in are swallowed immediately by the toad's impressive mouth, which is almost as wide as the toad's body is long.

*

Domesticated cats may have been taken from the wild, but they are no less expert at hunting than their big cat relatives. A study of more than two hundred domestic cats found that they caught and killed between ten and fifty animals a year. Their captures included mice, rats, frogs, other reptiles, goldfish, and forty-seven types of birds. The study also showed how subtle cats are at hunting. Cats with bells around their necks caught just as many animals as those without.

"I've Got You, I'm Under Your Skin":
How Parasites Kill Their Prey

All of nature is alive with parasites, small, predatory animals that literally live off larger animals. They are highly skilled at secreting themselves inside their hosts. For instance, one crustacean parasite sets up its home in a fish's mouth where it proceeds to eat the victim's tongue. It then takes over the tongue's job, receiving, tasting, and passing on food while taking all the best stuff for itself.

*

Brainwashing parasites can make their hosts do anything. One parasite that invades males of the American mayfly persuade the insect to change sex.

*

Some parasites castrate their victims.

When an invader gets into a host's body it is involved in a constant battle for its blood and tissue. It doesn't want to attack the host's vital organs or brain, so instead it targets something more expendable, the sexual organs. Among nature's most virulent castrators are wasps that invade caterpillars and barnacles that live inside a crab's shell.

*

Mind-altering hairworms that live inside grasshoppers pump their hosts with a cocktail of chemicals that persuades them to commit suicide by jumping into water.

The parasites then swim free, ready to start the search for a new host.

*

A parasite that invades rats forces the rodents to commit suicide by surrendering to their archenemy, the cat. Once the cat has eaten the rat, the parasite can continue its life cycle inside its new feline host.

*

A small liver fluke brainwashes ants into climbing to the top of blades of grass. It does this to give itself a better chance of being eaten by sheep, its ultimate host.

*

Some animals use chemicals to manipulate others to help them out. When it is a caterpillar, the large blue butterfly, known as *Maculinea rebeli,* produces chemicals similar to those of ant larvae to manipulate red ants into feeding, grooming, and protecting it.

*

A tapeworm can live for 18 years inside a human. In that time it can generate 10 billion eggs.

*

Not all parasites are clever, however. A fly that buries itself inside the tiger moth caterpillar brainwashes the insect into changing its tastes and eating a different plant. Unfortunately, the plant produces chemicals that are toxic and kill the parasite.

Liquids of Mass Destruction:
Deadly Weapons from the Animal Armory

A species of tropical ant catches its prey by using a device not dissimilar to a medieval torture rack. French scientists discovered the South American ant lures its victims into its trap, then stretches them out on the device built of plant fibers and fungus and pitted with holes in which other ants are waiting to pounce. They grab the legs and antennae of their captive then signal for the rest of the ant colony to swarm in. The device allows the ants to catch prey much bigger than themselves.

*

Bombardier beetles spray attackers with a jet of boiling chemicals. Scientists have discovered that the engine that projects the lethal weapon works along the same lines as the one that powered the German V1 buzz bomb in World War II.

*

Few creatures can match the firepower of the bombardier beetle, but a family of rain forest creatures, the part worm, part lobster onychophorans, comes close. They can fire powerful spurts of unpleasant, sticky slime from glands on their head. The slime acts like a quick-drying adhesive wrapping its prey in a web.

*

Of all jellyfish, the box jellyfish packs the most unpleasant punch. The Australian creature is the only species that causes the terrible Irukandji syndrome. In humans this manifests itself as a combination of intense pain, nausea, vomiting, disastrously high blood pressure, and a feeling of impending doom which can go on for days.

*

Worker termites guard the entrances to their nests, armed with spray guns attached to their noses. They use the weapon to fire at anteaters that threaten their nests.

*

Scorpions have an arsenal of poisons to choose from. When hunting for food they can dispense a weak venom that paralyzes insects like flies or moths. But when they are faced with threats from predators they bring out a much more powerful poison that can kill a large animal.

*

The European fire salamander is armed with a jet-powered gun it carries on its back. It tilts its body up and sprays a potent toxin via large skin glands when threatened. The poison attacks the victim's nervous system and renders its respiratory system paralyzed. Despite being only about 10 inches long, the salamander can fire its poisonous payload up to 6 feet.

*

The liquid a skunk fires at attackers from its behind is one of the most effective deterrents in the animal world. The stinking cocktail of chemicals clings to its victims and releases even more pungent smells when it reacts with water in the days that follow.

*

Spotted skunks do a handstand before launching their rancid payload. By lifting themselves up onto their front legs they can maximize the distance their anal secretions can fly. The spotted skunk can hit a target up to 13 feet away.

*

The mongoose can kill poisonous snakes. It can do this because, uniquely among mammals it is thought, the mongoose is immune to its victim's venom.

*

Hummingbirds are master swordsmen. The tiny birds are highly aggressive and will dive-bomb other birds that present a territorial threat. They are armed with a needle-sharp bill that allows them to stab their enemies, sometimes fatally.

*

Dragonflies are the stealth bombers of the insect world. The flies can pull off an extraordinary optical illusion that makes them appear to be stationary when they are in fact in full flight. This makes them very hard to spot and able to creep up on prey with deadly effect.

*

Archerfish fire spurts of water to dislodge insects.

*

Male cicadas competing for the affections of females have a clever trick for eliminating rivals. They fire sharp blasts of urine that knock them off the trees where mating is conducted.

*

Hippos conduct fierce territorial battles, especially in the lead-up to mating. Males stake their claims for territory by firing showers of feces at their rivals.

*

A rare red octopus has a unique trick for drawing in prey. The Atlantic-dwelling octopus has a row of raised, buttonlike suckers lined along each of its arms. It can make them flash on and off.

*

The eland, the biggest antelope, is equipped with a formidable weapon, a spiraled horn that can be as long as 4 feet and is capable of skewering a lion. Unfortunately, it also has a design flaw that leaves it vulnerable to one of its other main predators—human hunters. The eland's knees make a loud, clicking noise when it walks. Hunters can hear an eland walking from more than 100 yards.

*

A Mexican lizard has a unique weapon to fend off much bigger predators. When under attack, the regal horned lizard, which lives in the Sonoran desert, squirts blood. Even coyotes recoil in horror and retreat. The horned toad can perform a similar trick.

*

Some other lethal species: Electric eels can generate 600 volts of electricity, enough to kill a human. One of Australia's and the world's most lethal snakes, the inland taipan, delivers enough venom in one bite to kill 40,000 medium-sized rats. Little wonder it is more popularly known as the fierce snake. The diminutive blue poison frog from South America carries enough venom to kill 100 people. Just 2 micrograms of its venom can kill a human. The blue poison frog carries an average of 200 micrograms (more then 7 ounces) of venom.

The Japanese giant hornet has a venom so powerful it can dissolve human skin and tissue.

David 1, Goliath 0:
A Few of Nature's Mismatches

Elephants are afraid of honeybees. African elephants love stripping the bark of acacia trees to get the sap. But they will not eat the bark of trees where there are beehives, for fear of being attacked. Aggressive swarms of bees have been known to send elephants running for their lives.

*

Rattlesnakes don't frighten every animal. Californian ground squirrels in particular aren't impressed by the noisy predators. They taunt the snakes by lunging at them. They also kick sand in their faces.

*

Snakes are threatened by moving objects. This is why they rise out of baskets when they see a snake charmer's flute moving rhythmically above them. The music plays little part in tempting them out since they have very poor hearing.

*

The British brown hare can outfox even the fox. If it spots a fox approaching, the hare will stop, stand still, and signal its presence. Even though it can run much faster, it will remain there in full view of the fox rather than fleeing. The trick almost always works and the fox leaves the hare alone. Scientists think that once it knows it has been seen, the fox gives up on the idea of chasing the hare. The hare knows this and uses its tactic to save itself the effort of having to run.

*

The bombardier beetle is one of the most fearsome creatures on earth. It doesn't frighten every creature, however.

Some toads are so quick they can flick out their adhesive tongues, capture the beetle, and pop it in their mouths before the bombardier has had time to fire its payload of boiling chemicals. Some spiders, too, have the ability to wrap the beetles in an absorbent silk web that protects them from poisons.

The most effective counter-bombardier measures, however, are those of the grasshopper mouse. It swiftly grabs the beetle and performs the equivalent of a rugby spear tackle, upending the beetle and burying its deadly rear end in the ground. As the beetle frantically fires its poison into the earth, the mouse enjoys a leisurely meal.

*

Hares have single-handedly attacked teams of huskies. Reports of an attack in Norway described the "large and aggressive" hare leaping into a pack of dogs and hitting them on the nose. The baffled dogs froze and simply stared at the hare. The hare stared back unfazed.

The Escape Artists:
Nature's Great Survivors

Lizards can discard their tails at will. If a predator sinks its teeth into the tail, the lizard will simply cast it off and run away.

A variety of sea creatures are also capable of jettisoning limbs in a crisis. Among those capable of pulling off the trick are crabs, lobsters, and starfish. Starfish can survive as long as they maintain one of their five hands. If a lobster jettisons one of its claws, the missing limb does its best to help it make a getaway by tightening its grip on the attacker. All three creatures are capable of regenerating new limbs over time.

*

Few animals have such drastic self-defense mechanisms as the sea cucumber.

A relative of the starfish and sea urchin, cucumbers, as their name suggests, are shaped like the vegetable and are not much more nimble. They live attached to rocks on the ocean bed where they are constantly under threat from fishy predators.

To preserve themselves when under attack the cucumber commits an act science has called autonomy. This involves their blowing out a major part of their anatomy, usually through the front or rear of their body. Often it is their intestines they jettison, sometimes it is their lungs. Some eject their digestive system and their gonads. One species of cucumber forces itself to have a hernia, and ejects its digestive system along with sticky tubes that tangle themselves around their attacker. Whatever is launched, the cucumber's spectacular act of self-mutilation acts as decoy to the predators who assume their victim has exploded. As long as it keeps 5 percent of its original body, the cucumber will be able to regenerate itself.

*

Nature's ultimate escape artist may be the mother-of-pearl caterpillar. When faced with a predator the caterpillar hurls itself backwards at 39 times its walking speed, throwing in half a dozen somersaults for good measure.

*

A tiny ocean snail is the only creature known to have a metal coat of armor. The 2-inch snail was only discovered in 2001 and doesn't have a name. It has protective scales made from metallic sulphides including iron pyrite, otherwise known as fool's gold. The armor is thought to protect it from a rival snail that fires poison darts.

*

The three-banded armadillo can roll itself into an almost perfect ball when under attack. It tucks in its ears, and its tail and head come together so that only its armor-plated exterior is visible. Its more vulnerable underside is then safely protected.

*

The zebra's stripes may be one of nature's subtlest forms of camouflage. Scientists think the stripes echo the "waviness" of the air on the African savannah when temperatures are high. From a distance of a few hundred yards, zebras seem to blend into the shimmering horizon. The stripes also act as protection against blood-sucking insects.

*

The ostrich doesn't bury its head in the sand. What it does do, however, is lie down on the ground with its neck outstretched. It does this to avoid being spotted by predators.

*

The underside of some Heike crabs bears a striking resemblance to the face of an ancient Japanese warrior. Hence the species's nickname: the samurai crab. Japanese tradition has it that the creatures carry the spirit of the long-gone swordsmen, so captured crabs with samurai faces are returned to the sea.

*

Amazonian ants know how to parachute to safety. The ants live high in the treetops, up to 98 feet above the ground, and are vulnerable to gusts of wind. But if they are blown off they turn feetfirst and guide themselves back to the tree. Most march back to where they were blown off course within ten minutes.

*

When threatened, the pufferfish swallows as much water as it can so as to blow up like a balloon. Its size and the spikes on its exterior make it too big and unpalatable for predators to swallow.

*

When a dolphin is sick or injured, its cries of distress summon immediate aid from other dolphins, who try to support it to the surface so that it can breathe.

*

The seemingly indestructible cockroach can live for 9 days without its head. Even this pales next to the chicken, which has been known to live for 18 months headless. A chicken named Mike from Colorado survived that long after the axman who beheaded him left a small section of his brain stem intact. His owner fed him with an eyedropper, which he used to drop food and drink directly into his gullet.

Throughout, Mike continued to peck vainly for food and when he tried to make a crowing noise simply gurgled. He eventually choked to death when he ate a kernel of corn.

And the Oscar Goes to . . . :
How Animals Act Their Way Out
of Trouble

Mimicry is a common form of self-defense in animals. Many species are able to convince others they are something they are not. On an island in Indonesia, for instance, inhabitants live in dread of a small snake, known as ular kepala dua, although it is only about 8 inches long and has no venom. The snake has a tail with markings similar to those of a cobra. When it is threatened the snake buries its head, flattens and raises its tail, and begins to strike like its poisonous relative. How it learned to imitate the more dangerous snake is a mystery, as the cobra isn't a native of the island.

Similarly, Californian gopher snakes pretend they are rattlesnakes. Faced with danger, they spread out the back of their heads, hiss loudly, and vibrate their tails. This is enough to frighten off most potential predators.

*

A Brazilian hawk moth caterpillar has a similar technique for defending itself. When threatened, the caterpillar inflates its thorax so that it looks like the head of a dangerous snake.

*

Even cobras exaggerate their threat. They have hoods that can expand like an umbrella and make them seem much larger and more aggressive than they really are.

*

Frogs bluff. In a tactic that is thought to be designed to put off predators, they produce deep croaks that suggest they are bigger than they are.

*

Masters of illusion, stick insects not only blend in by looking like twigs, but they also produce eggs that look and even smell like seeds to deter predators from detecting and eating them.

*

A species of caterpillar, the *Nemoria,* avoids predators by disguising themselves as their favorite food. In the spring they pretend to be oak catkins, in summer they imitate twigs.

*

The octopus is a master of disguise. An Australian species is capable of imitating seaweed, while an Indonesian octopus wraps itself up into a ball, then rolls along the ocean floor. Biologists believe the latter is pretending to be a coconut being swept along by the current.

*

Another striped octopus is a master at improvisation and is capable of imitating a host of other creatures, particularly poisonous ones. The creature can spread its limbs to look like a toxic lionfish and flatten its body and undulate along the seabed like a poisonous flatfish. It reserves its best trick for when it is attacked by its great rival, the damselfish. The octopus puts six of its legs into a hole, keeping the remaining two out so as to look like a deadly sea snake. Scientists believe the remarkable actor may also be able to do a credible impersonation of a sand anemone and a stingray.

*

Butterflies bluff their way out of life-or-death situations. Faced with its chief predator, the blue tit, the peacock butterfly flashes the eye-spots on its wings. The attackers are momentarily confused, unsure whether they are facing a blinking owl or another large bird who might attack first. While the tit hesitates, the butterfly escapes.

PART SIX

WORK, REST, AND PLAY: ANIMAL LIFESTYLES

No matter how strange they may seem to us, the lifestyles to which animals have evolved are successful and have been so for thousands of years. (Those that aren't are on their way to extinction.) As with human lifestyles, the most successful animals balance work, rest, and play.

Six (or Eight) Feet Under:
Some Animal Occupations

Wrasse fish are gifted masseurs. The wrasse live off dead bits of skin and the parasites they are allowed to clean from the bodies of other fish. If a wrasse nips its client's skin, the client will leave and find another, more careful cleaner. So the wrasse learn to give their customers enjoyable back rubs to make sure their clients return again and again.

*

Some bees act as undertakers, removing dead workers from the hive. They are believed to be a higher class of bee than ordinary workers and are developmentally more advanced.

*

Some young birds work as au pairs. Rather than leaving the nest to breed, one-year-old Florida scrub jays stay at home with their families. They defend and clean the nest and help with the raising of their younger siblings. The behavior is highly unusual in birds but isn't quite the unselfish act it seems. Rather than risking everything by leaving home for an uncertain life elsewhere, they are waiting for a suitable partner to arrive. As soon as a mate arrives they quit the au pair's job and flee.

*

Chimpanzees practice dentistry. Groups of chimps have been observed using pieces of wood as toothpicks to clean each other's teeth. While the patient chimp sits still, the dentist chimp uses the toothpick to carefully remove food particles from its teeth.

*

Birds and bees are not the only creatures to pollinate flowers. Gerbils perform the role for a rare species of African lily.

*

Kangaroos are expert well diggers. They can excavate holes as deep as 4 feet in order to access water.

*

Butterflies are chemists. African milkweed butterflies are capable of mixing more than two hundred different chemicals, many of which are unknown to the rest of nature.

*

South America's only bear, the so-called spectacled bear, does an important job as a forestry worker. The bear disperses the seeds of laurel trees through its droppings, ensuring supplies of this much-valued hardwood are maintained.

*

The old saying "Hard work never killed anyone" doesn't apply to bumblebees. A study of Canadian insects compared the life spans of worker bees that made lots of trips to forage for food with lazier bees that stayed at home.

The hardworking bees died significantly younger—mainly because their wings wore out.

*

To produce 1 pound of honey a honeybee would need to make around 10 million collection trips.

Workers of the World:
Nature's Jack-of-All-Trades

No creature is as versatile or as hardworking as the ant, the jack-of-all-trades of the insect world. Here are a few of the many jobs it carries out:

Armed Guards: Small leaf-cutter ants ride shotgun on the backs of bigger ants. The small, lookout ants watch out for predators as the bigger ants carry leaves back to the colony.

Gardeners: Nature's most green-fingered creatures, ants have been cultivating gardens of tasty fungus for 50 million years, according to scientists. In that time they have learned to delegate a range of jobs.

A special team of leaf-cutter ants, for instance, performs weeding. Because the ants rely on the fungus gardens for their food, they have to be careful that the right kinds of fungus grow there. Ants on weeding duty remove infected parts of the garden and take it to their equivalent of a compost heap. The ants also tidy up the garden.

Ants have also developed a range of pesticides to protect their gardens. Some ants carry a potent antibiotic bacteria in special pockets on their bodies that help control a parasite that can ruin their fungus harvest. They have also developed pesticides that clear their gardens of unwanted plants.

Amazonian ants clear patches of land local tribesmen call "devil gardens" containing only one tree species. They keep the gardens clear of other overgrowth by spraying unwanted plants with their own homemade herbicide: formic acid.

MILKMAIDS: Females belonging to some species milk aphids by stroking them with their antennae or front legs. Rather like a cow being coaxed to produce milk from its udder, the aphid produces droplets of sugary honeydew which the ants store in their abdomens. When their abdomens are full, the ants return to the nest to regurgitate the honeydew for the rest of the nest to share.

MILLERS: The largest workers in armies of harvesting ants, these ants mill the seeds that are brought back to the nest by smaller workers. They use their big mandibles to peel the outer coat of the seed to get to the nutrient-rich center.

TEACHERS: When foraging for food, a mature *temnothorax* ant may carry an apprentice ant along with it. The teacher uses a technique scientists have called "tandem running" to show the student the right path to take on future food runs.

The teacher shows great patience. If the student stops every now and again to familiarize itself with the surroundings, the teacher waits. The student then taps the teacher on the hind legs and abdomen when it is ready to move on. If the student drops too far behind, the teacher slows down and waits for it. It takes the teacher four times longer to get to the food, but scientists believe the loss to the colony in terms of this single journey is more than compensated for by having another ant introduced to the correct route.

UNDERTAKERS: Leaf-cutter ants also act as undertakers. A team of ants is delegated the job of carrying dead members of the colony to the compost heap it keeps near its fungus garden.

Skilled Labor:
Animals That Use Tools

Chimpanzees use tool kits. Scientists have observed them use a range of different tools, including "chisels," a "hole puncher," and a dipping instrument to gain access to a supply of honey in a beehive.

*

As they wade their way into lakes or pools, gorillas test the depth with sticks. Photographs have been taken of apes guiding themselves through water using a yard-long piece of wood.

*

Ants use their equivalent of electric knives. The knives are powered by stridulation, the same action ants use to squeak messages, in which they rub together two different parts of their hindmost body section. In this case the vibrations make their jaws buzz. This makes it easier for them to tear their way through leaves, flowers, stems, and other plant tissue to be carried back to the nest.

*

Hornets use the insect equivalent of a level to build their geometrically perfect comb nests. The hornets use tiny crystals which somehow act to tell them at what angle to build the walls and roofs of their cells. The tool is even more impressive because it functions in the pitch-black conditions that hornets work in. Scientists themselves are still in the dark about exactly how it works.

*

The New Caledonian crow, native to the Pacific island of the same name, is recognized as the only animal that makes its own tools. Scientific studies have recorded the crow making a variety of implements capable of retrieving food. These include hook-shaped tools made from plant material which are used to extract grubs from inside logs and branches. In a scientific study, a New Caledonian crow spontaneously bent a piece of wire into a hook in order to get food out from a tube in which it had been hidden.

The super-clever crows even run research and development centers to improve their toolmaking. A study found that communities of crows seem to share knowledge about their work. Crows learn from each other which designs work and which do not and modify their tools accordingly.

*

Dolphins use sponges. Bottle-nosed dolphins carry the sponges in their mouths while searching for food. Scientists think they use them to scoop prey out of places that are otherwise hard to reach.

*

Birds of prey use rocks to break giant eggs. Egyptian vultures have been observed using various tricks to break open hard-shelled eggs. If the egg is relatively small the vulture will grasp it in its beak, take off, and drop it on the ground from a height. But if the vulture comes across a giant egg too large to be moved, such as that of an ostrich, it uses a different technique. The vulture will drop stones from great heights until it cracks the egg. Australian black-breasted buzzards have been observed using the same method to break open emu eggs.

No Place Like Home:
How Animals Find Their Domestic Bliss

European starlings are very house-proud. They decorate their nests with a collection of leaves that they rearrange regularly. They also carry out a major spring cleaning each year.

*

Bats build wigwams. The Panamanian bats make the tepees from leaves that they neatly lay together to form a cone shape.

*

Parakeets live in apartment blocks. The South American monk parakeet builds a series of covered nests that are stacked on top of each other. The tower blocks can have as many as fifteen stories.

*

Termites construct the most impressive insect homes. The largest was found in Australia. It was 100 feet in diameter at the base and 20 feet high. An African mound with a smaller base of 10 feet reached 42 feet in height.

*

Some beetles live inside centrally heated plants. In French Guiana, for instance, scarab beetles live inside flowers that maintain a temperature four degrees warmer than outside during the night. The flowers provide the rent-free accommodation for a reason, however. While inside, the beetles feed on the flowers' pollen, fertilizing it in the process.

*

As you'd expect of the bird that is the symbol of the United States, the bald eagle builds its home on a large scale. Pairs of eagles will return to the same nest from year to year and are constantly adding to it. The largest nest on record was 9½ feet wide and 20 feet high. It weighed more than 2 tons.

*

Rock-moving wrasse fish are the nomads of the deep and build new homes every night. The wrasse collect assorted bits of rubble off the seafloor, then turn their bric-a-brac into a small den. They spend the night there, then strike camp and move on the next morning.

*

Birds decorate their nests with a healthy potpourri.

Many species, including hummingbirds, line their nests with aromatic leaves. Scientists have learned that they perform different functions. The yarrow leaf, for instance, keeps mosquitoes away. Other plants kill off bacteria, while some simply act as a shield from the sun.

*

Rats decorate their nests with bay leaves. Scientists think they place the aromatic leaves near where they sleep so as to fumigate their homes against parasites.

*

House-proud termites keep their homes clean by using mothballs. The small deposits of naphthalene, the same substance used to keep human wardrobes free from moths, keep pests like fire ants away from the termite mound.

*

Some animals prefer the smell of fresh dung. Waxbills protect their nests from predators by scenting it with the dried feces of much bigger, scarier animals. African birds collect the droppings of big carnivores from the savannah, then sprinkle it around their homes. Other waxbills collect dung-impregnated feathers from larger birds. In both cases, the smell persuades predators it mightn't be such a good idea to attack the waxbills' nests.

*

Burrowing owls collect dung outside their nests not to deter predators but to attract their favorite meal, dung beetles. The dung acts as bait. The owls wait patiently, sitting still like fishermen until their prey arrives.

*

Hermit crabs house swap. The crabs live in mobile homes made from the shells of dead mollusks they dig up on the ocean floor. Hermits are notoriously picky, however. Crabs that aren't satisfied with their homes get together and exchange shells with other crabs.

*

Beavers create their own water parks.

They dig channels and dam streams with rocks, branches, and mud to create networks of ponds. They then construct lodges made of mud and sticks with underwater entrances to deter predators. Opinion is divided on whether this is good or bad for the environment. Some argue beavers play a major role in their ecosystems by creating ponds where many species of plants and animals can thrive.

Others, however, blame them for contributing to global warming. Beaver communities lead to flooding and the buildup of sediment and rotting vegetation. This produces what climatologists have called "tremendous" levels of greenhouse gases like methane and carbon dioxide.

*

Some female wasps can't be bothered with all the effort of homemaking. The paper wasps save their energy for raising their young by letting other females of the species build homes, then stealing them.

Beauty and the Beasts:
Health, Hygiene, and Beauty
in the Animal World

Some birds put on makeup. During courtship, migrating sandpipers naturally produce a wax that coats their wings. The wax makeup is thought to attract partners, but also helps the birds when they are incubating their eggs.

*

Egyptian vultures beautify themselves by using a unique facial product—other animals' feces. Having a brightly colored face is attractive to the vultures, so the birds eat the droppings of cows, sheep, and goats, which are rich in a pigment called lutein. Eaten in enough quantities, the lutein turns the vultures' faces from a pale white to a glowing yellow, a signal that they are not only handsome, but also virile enough to cope with all the parasites they will have ingested from their diet of dung.

*

Many birds groom themselves with an ant-i-biotic cream. They capture and crush ants, then rub the mashed-up insects into their feathers so as to release the antibiotic secretions they carry inside them. Birds that don't have access to ants make do with other body lotions. Some use crushed millipedes, others marigolds. Some birds have even been seen rubbing themselves down with the tobacco from the discarded butt of a cigarette. All apparently have antibacterial properties.

*

Animals make their own hair conditioner.

North American brown bears store up on osha roots, which they chew into a pulp. They then rub the frothy mixture into their coats. Scientists think it keeps their pelts healthy and free from parasites. In a similar vein, the Panamanian coatis, a relative of the raccoon, groom themselves with the sap from an indigenous tree, the Trattinnickia.

*

Monkeys have their own form of insect repellant. The capuchin monkeys smear themselves with a body cream containing toxic chemicals to fend off pesky insects. The capuchins make the repellant from millipedes that they catch, crush, and then mash into a paste.

*

Monkeys get a chemical buzz from being groomed that is similar to the high humans get from taking opiates like heroin.

Ringtailed lemurs have comblike teeth. They use them for grooming each other.

*

Long hair has never gone out of fashion among male lions. The longer, more lustrous, and dark a lion's mane, the more attractive he is to females—and the more other males fear him. There are good reasons for this. Lions with long, dark manes tend to have higher testosterone levels, carry fewer injuries, and are generally fitter and better nourished. Even the king of the jungle has an Achilles' heel, however. Infrared studies have shown big manes generate huge amounts of heat and this can drain a male's energy when it is out on the open savannah.

*

But being bald may not be a total disadvantage in the lion world.

Male lions that live in Tsavo National Park in Kenya are unusual in that they have sparse blond hair, a beard, a hairy chest, and sideburns—but no mane. Despite this, studies have shown they have an active sex life and tend to have an entire pride of females to themselves. Lions with manes often have to share their mates with one to three other males in the pride. This has led some to wonder whether, rather like in the human world, thinning on top may in fact be a symbol of virility.

*

Most birds are fastidious about cleanliness, but the male rock ptarmigan, a native of the frozen tundra of Antarctica, deliberately smears itself in mud. Predictably, the reason is linked to sex. To avoid predators like falcons and blend in with the changing seasonal landscape, ptarmigans naturally have a white color during the snowy winter. This coat molts to reveal a more mottled feather color during summer, when the snows melt and the landscape turns browner. The males deliberately dirty themselves during the winter so that they stand out against the snow. By removing their camouflage like this, scientists believe the males advertise their macho qualities to potential females. Once they have found a mate, the ptarmigans wash themselves down to blend in with the white snowy wasteland once more.

*

Crabs keep their shells clean by burying themselves in sand. Once submerged they use the sand to scrub off the bacteria and mini-barnacles that accumulate on their backs.

*

Porcupines sharpen their teeth on rocks.

*

Animals watch their diets. They adjust their eating habits to make sure they get the right nutritional balance. Among those animals proven to be picky eaters are ground beetles and spiders. Each were given diets skewed toward either fat (lipids) or proteins. When they were then given a choice of choosing either lipids or proteins, they went for food that compensated for the previous imbalance.

Offered a range of foods by biologists, trout opted for a high-protein diet and avoided fats and carbohydrates.

Scientists think carnivorous animals eat a balanced diet, too. Wolves and cats who eat carcasses may concentrate on different parts of the body for different nutrients, chewing bones, for instance, to provide themselves with calcium.

*

Spiny lobsters are extremely health and hygiene conscious. They also have good taste. At the end of a meal they clean their antennae by drawing them through their mouths, which contains tiny cleaning brushes. They are particularly sensitive to any traces of monosodium glutamate, the unhealthy flavoring found in Chinese fast food, which occurs naturally on the seabed. At the first sign of this they start cleaning themselves.

*

Hippopotamus sweat is a red-orange color. Scientists believe it may act as an antibiotic sunscreen.

Rip Van Winkles:

How Animals Get Their Heads Down

Several animals, including the rat and the platypus, have been found to experience REM, rapid eye movement, suggesting they experience dreams.

A pilot whale has also been observed having an REM dream. It lasted for six minutes.

*

The expression "half-asleep" applies to many species.

To protect itself from predators, for instance, a bottle-nosed dolphin sleeps using one half of its brain at a time. It shuts down one half and closes one eye, while keeping the other half and eye open. It reverses the process every two hours or so and generally spends a third of each day in this state. Marine biologists believe this catnapping allows the dolphin to retain control of its blowhole and also to know when it needs to surface for air. If the dolphin shut down both sides of the brain while swimming, scientists think it would drown.

*

Ducks have a sophisticated technique for protecting each other when they sleep. Ducks on the outer edges of a group sleep with only half their brain and with one eye open. This allows the ducks in the middle of the group to

close down both hemispheres of their brain in order to get
a good night's sleep.

*

Cockatiels and penguins have also been observed sleeping
with one eye open, suggesting they, too, only half-sleep.
The albatross is believed to be capable of using this technique most effectively of all. By shutting down half its
brain and leaving the other half to act as an automatic pilot,
the seabird can fly enormous distances, almost ten thousand miles in a single flight.

*

Giraffes sleep standing up. The time required to get up
after they collapse their legs to lie down is such that they
become sitting targets for predators.

*

Rip Van Winkle by name: gastropods such as snails,
limpets, and British winkles are thought to sleep longer
than any other species. Some snails can nod off for three
years.

*

Bears, gorillas, and dogs have been heard snoring at New
York's Bronx Zoo.

    Snakes are noisy sleepers, too. A hognose snake has
been beard snoring.

*

Wombats hunt by night and sleep by day. They do so lying
on their backs with their feet in the air. They also snore.

*

Yawning is contagious among chimpanzees. If one starts,
others generally follow.

*

Insects don't sleep in the human and mammal sense. Scorpions, cockroaches, honeybees, fruit flies, and wasps do fall quiet every night, however. They also breathe less often and tend to droop their antennae.

*

Animals that eat meat tend to sleep the most, while those that graze sleep the least. So while a meat-eating brown bat sleeps for 20 hours a day, a grazing horse only sleeps for 2 hours. The reason is obvious. Zebras, for instance, have little time to sleep. To get the energy they need to survive on the open savannah, they must forage for grass for between 14 and 20 hours per day.

The rule doesn't apply to all animals. Koalas, for instance, sleep for most of the day even though they graze mainly on eucalyptus leaves. This may be because the leaves can be poisonous if eaten to excess. So, starved of the nutrition necessary for an active life, koalas conserve energy by sleeping. Life during their waking hours isn't much more exciting either. They spend the time either eating or resting.

*

Do bears urinate in the woods? Certainly not during hibernation. During the long winter sleep, bears go five to seven months without relieving themselves.

*

Shrimp can play dead. If oxygen levels are low in the water, brine shrimp are able to shut down their systems and enter a unique, deathlike state in which their body uses no energy. When the conditions are right, they are "reborn" weeks, months, or even years later.

*

Baby painted turtles in Canada survive their first winters by transforming themselves into ice cubes. Half their body fluid turns to ice and their bodies become stiff to the touch. The hatchlings then thaw out in the spring, ready to start proper growth.

*

The only mammal able to routinely tolerate subzero temperatures during hibernation in the frozen tundra is thought to be the arctic ground squirrel.

*

Even tropical monkeys hibernate. A Madagascan fat-tailed lemur spends the winter curled up inside a hole in a tree.

Moose Surf, Dragons Play Frisbee:
How Animals Get Stressed,
and How They Unwind

Hamsters get depressed in winter.

A study showed that hamsters that spent their early days in an environment where there was less daylight were more inclined to be anxious and depressed than those who saw more of the sun.

*

Fish get stressed by the sound of boats.

Fish release a hormone called cortisol when agitated. Studies have found the sound of rumbling engines produces high levels of cortisol, particularly in species like carp, perch, and gudgeon that are fished commercially.

*

Television makes chickens calmer. Scientists discovered that battery hens became less anxious and aggressive

when they watched random images on the box for ten minutes a day. The most relaxing images were fish and flying toasters.

*

Chickens have also been tested to see how they react to human faces. The faces they preferred were "consistent with human sexual preferences." In other words, they like beautiful people best.

*

Monkeys enjoy pottery. Given lumps of clay and paints, capuchin monkeys have been observed turning the clay into shapes which they then decorate to a standard similar to that of an 18- to 24-month-old human child. Like humans, some monkeys are more "artistic" than others.

*

Fish sunbathe. The Australian bluefin tuna will spend hours rolling itself over onto its side to catch the sun's rays as it swims along. Marine biologists believe it is warming itself so as to grow bigger and stronger.

Ring-tailed lemurs also love sunbathing. Highly sociable animals, lemurs sit together in groups with their arms outstretched to soak up the sun's rays.

*

Lizards prefer putting their feet up and enjoying the good life. Studies showed that, given the choice, iguanas preferred to remain in the warmth of their homes rather than heading out into the cold in search of food. They also showed signs of getting positive stimulation from being in a warm environment, one of the first creatures to display signs of sensory pleasure.

*

At the end of a hard day's work, male monarch butterflies need a drink. Their tipple of choice is water, which they drink in the form of dewdrops.

*

Locusts lose all their inhibitions if they are touched repeatedly on the back of their legs. Shy insects are transformed into gregarious ones when this happens.

*

The best way to calm a stressed sheep is by introducing it to another sheep. Introducing another animal, such as a goat, does little to calm its nerves.

*

Cows enjoy listening to classical music. Music can increase milk yields in dairy cattle, but different styles produce different results. Cows that were played Beethoven's *Pastoral Symphony* produced 3 percent more milk than cows that were played no music at all. The sound of less soothing music, such as Bananarama's 1986 hit "Venus," lowered the cows' lactation rates, however.

*

Snails are the scourge of human gardeners. But an American snail, the marsh periwinkle, tends to its own garden. The snail allotment is made of fungus, which it feeds by eating marsh grass.

*

Dragons love playing with Frisbees. While growing up at the National Zoo in Washington, a baby komodo dragon named Kraken regularly played with a range of toys, from plastic rings and a shoe, to a bucket, a tin can, and—her personal favorite—a Frisbee. Kraken would pick the objects up in her mouth or swipe at them with her paws, just like a playful young puppy or kitten. The dragon even spontaneously joined in a game of tug-of-war, reaching up to snatch a handkerchief from a keeper's rear pocket then tugging at it with her mouth while he pulled at the other end. Her games surprised animal behaviorists who hadn't expected reptiles to display such a playful side.

*

Moose surf. After heavy rains in Norway, a large moose was observed surfing down the raging waters of the Namsen River on a large chunk of ice.

*

Otters love tobogganing.

In studies they have been observed repeatedly sliding down snowy slopes.

PART SEVEN

SOCIAL ANIMAL:
HOW CREATURES LIVE TOGETHER

All animals are equal, but some animals are
more equal than others.
—George Orwell,
Animal Farm, 1945

A few thousand years' worth of history has taught us
what happens when you stick a collection of humans
together. Some will get along just fine; others, however,
will want to compete, argue, dominate, and, if absolutely
necessary, kill those who don't toe the line. It's no different in the animal world. Different species have evolved
their own versions of monarchy and mob rule, police
states and fascist regimes. In many places, in fact, some
animals will do anything to be more equal than others.

All for One, and One for All:
How Animals Look Out for Each Other

Prairie dogs live in such a friendly society they greet each other with a kiss.

A relative of the squirrel, the prairie dog is one of the most sociable rodents. When two dogs meet they greet each other by touching their lips together. They do this with their mouths open and teeth exposed. Often their kiss extends to touching teeth and even locking their incisors together for about ten seconds.

*

Some ants behave like the Three Musketeers, upholding the principle "all for one, and one for all." The red fire ant, in particular, forms one of the tightest-knit groups in the natural world. When one member of the community is threatened, every other member of the community comes to the rescue.

An endangered ant sets off an aromatic alarm in which it releases a powerful pheromone. This alerts all the other ants to attack simultaneously, each delivering a powerful sting.

This is bad news for any creature that is attacked by a swarm of ants. Fire ants stinging in unison are capable of killing animals as big as a small deer foal. Humans too have been known to die from concentrated attacks.

Their egalitarian instincts do cause the ants problems, however. The ants are so small they can enter electrical appliances. If they get electrocuted their pheromone alarms are set off and thousands more ants pile in to help, only to get themselves sizzled. The domino effect can be spectacular. Fire ant attacks have been known to cause electrical blackouts in entire towns.

*

Penguins dive in teams of up to eleven. They act as dive buddies watching out for each other.

*

Most cats are, by nature, solitary creatures. Of the thirty-nine or so known feline species, the most sociable are male cheetahs, who tend to form close ties to their brothers, and female lions who remain in matriarchal prides.

*

The nicest animal in the world may be a bird called the Arabian babbler.

Babblers operate as an unusually tight-knit community. They watch out for each other, feed each other, lovingly preen each other when grooming; they even cuddle up closely to keep each other warm at nighttime. Babblers also put the collective good first by letting only a few dominant members of each community breed, then dutifully pulling together to raise the young.

Their behavior is so unusually kind and generous scientists simply can't believe they are so unselfish. Babbler society is strictly hierarchical, with males and older birds at the top of the pile. Some think that, a bit like humans who throw money around at charity events to show off their social standing, babblers may use their niceness as a way of establishing their status, too.

*

Sperm whales may have the most egalitarian society of all. Studies have found no evidence of dominance or hierarchies, something that is almost universally present in land-living mammals. All members of a unit of sperm whales are happy in each other's company and will work together for the collective good. This closeness may explain why many whales are sometimes found stranded on beaches together.

*

South American spiders are more sociable than species from elsewhere in the world. Spiders are generally solitary insects, but one species from Ecuador likes to hang out with each other—they gather in groups of a dozen or so at a time around communal webs.

*

The world's largest insect colony is in southern Europe and stretches from the Atlantic coast of Spain to Italy. The colony contains billions of ants. The irony is the insects aren't even European. They originate in Argentina.

*

It may never really rain cats and dogs, but it does rain ants. Members of one species of ant, the northern wood ant, leap into the air by the hundreds when they feel threatened by birds, forming a dark shower as they fall to safety.

*

Family values are alive and well in the world of the meerkat.

Aggression is rare within groups of meerkats and there

is also very little sexual tension within the community as only the dominant male and female mate. The rest of the group are happy to forgo their own chances of reproducing for the benefit of the community as a whole. (They also know their genes are effectively being passed on as everyone in the group is related and they are equipped with a heightened sense of smell to detect meerkats who are not.) Instead, they help the parents with feeding and babysitting, or they act as foragers or lookouts, guarding against attacks from predators like hawks. The more close-knit the meerkat family, the better life is, especially for pups. Studies have shown that meerkats raised in large, cooperative groups grow up to be fatter because of the extra food the additional adults bring to the group.

Other animals that display similar, tight-knit behavior include African wild dogs, chimpanzees, naked mole rats, lions, and birds like kookaburras, pied kingfishers, and Seychelles warblers.

*

An Australian lizard, the black rock skink, is thought to be the only reptile that lives in a traditional nuclear family. Such is their belief in the benefits of family life, they also adopt orphaned or half-sibling skinks into their groups.

*

Ducks huddle together for protection, with the ducks on the perimeter expected to act as lookouts. Flocks can be as large as 2,000 ducks.

*

Prairie dogs have their own departments of homeland security.

The rodents live in colonies of more than 2,000 but squeeze themselves into an area less than an acre. They dig up to 100 burrows, 15 feet deep, each with two entrances in case they need to escape from predators.

Sentries are posted at most of these entrances and will signal when threats appear.

*

Birds of a feather stick together, particularly if they are Baikal teal. The world's entire population of the wildfowl, which breeds in Siberia, migrates en masse each winter to South Korea. A quarter million teal gather together and make the journey south.

*

Animals have been known to form the oddest of couples. Cats and dogs, for instance, have both adopted injured birds. A cat in Porto Alegre, Brazil, reportedly raised a bird as if it were its own after discovering it unable to fly after falling from its nest. The two formed an unlikely alliance, sharing the same eating bowl and the bird adopting a meaty diet. The bird even allowed itself to be used by the cat as bait to trap other, healthier birds.

In China, a Chihuahua adopted an orphaned chick. The dog acted as the chick's surrogate parent, watching over it and picking it up in its mouth and taking it safely home when it risked getting into trouble.

*

Dogs will allow the offspring of other species to suckle from them. A kitten and a pair of tiger cubs have been observed feeding off the breasts of dogs in China.

*

When a hog lost its longtime soul mate, it found solace in the unlikely form of an antelope. The hog moved in with the bongo, the largest forest antelope, at a zoo in Los Angeles. The two became inseparable, sleeping together, cuddling, and nuzzling romantically.

Government, for the Animals, by the Animals: Politics, Power, and Police States

Animals have gotten closer than humans to creating utopias in which millions live together in harmony and equality. To do so, however, they have learned that controlling those who don't obey the rules is essential.

Insects, for instance, run strictly controlled societies that resemble police states. Those who become enemies of the state by transgressing their laws face harsh punishments.

In wasp, bee, and ant communities the queen's authority is absolute. She—not the workers—must lay all the female eggs in the nest. The punishment for breaking this law is severe.

If a worker honeybee comes across a stray egg, for instance, it will conduct a thorough investigation. If the bee detective decides the egg hasn't been laid by the queen it will eat it.

Wasps are even tougher. If they discover female members of their nest laying their own eggs, they immediately form a vigilante gang, grab the criminal, and deliver a series of painful stings.

Workers act as a police force in many societies, but in

smaller ones it is often the queen herself who patrols the nest to make sure no one is defying her authority.

Among a species of Brazilian ants, the queen keeps an iron grip on her status as the alpha female by marking rivals with a chemical. This is a signal for a gang of subordinate ants to mete out the punishment.

Honeybees run prisons. South African bees build prisons to capture their main predator, the tanklike hive beetle. They work as a team to force invading beetles into the small, cracklike cells. Once captured, the jail beetles are watched over by warden bees, who specialize in the task.

*

Badly behaved monkeys feel the long arm of the law. A study of a community of pigtail macaques discovered that they have a group of elderly supervisor monkeys. When these police monkeys briefly left the community a mini–crime wave broke out—violence shot up, fighting cliques formed, and normal social behavior like grooming and playing disappeared. Order was only restored when the police monkeys returned to discipline the errant apes.

*

Some insects will not be willingly subjugated, however, so slavery is alive and well in the ant world. Some twenty species of ant kidnap other species and press-gang them into forced labor. The slave ants are even forced to take part in raids on their own species.

Some slave-making ants are more brutal than others. Some of the toughest ants come from New York. Scientists studied the New York ants' behavior compared to that of their country cousins from West Virginia. The New

Yorkers captured more ants during raids and also killed more queens. Their success is in part due to special "bouncer" ants who guard the entrance to the invaded nest. No ants are allowed to leave or enter without the bouncer's permission. The ant allows adults to leave if they surrender any young ants they may be carrying.

Unsurprisingly, however, New York ants are less likely to accept slavery without a fight. They fight back more than country ants and sting invading slave-makers more too.

*

One European ant captures nests of slaves single-handedly. Despite being tiny, this European queen ant conquers nests of much bigger ants by fixing herself underneath the reigning queen and slowly strangling her to death. The old queen's workers do nothing to help her, and within three weeks the new queen has taken over.

*

It may look like a single creature, but the Portuguese man-of-war jellyfish is in fact a colony of single-cell organisms that work together. The individual sections of the man-of-war divide labor up among themselves, with some devoted to movement, some to feeding, and some to distributing food around the network. Some parts can break free while the main body remains stuck to the seabed. The collective comes together when it is threatened by predators or wants to colonize new territory.

*

Some dolphins are expert politicians.

Studies of dolphin communities have revealed that a large pod is made up of a collection of smaller groupings.

These groupings are kept together by a small number of highly sociable, influential individuals. These dolphins spend time with the different factions and stimulate interaction between them. If these dolphins leave the pod, it breaks up. If they return, it gets back together again.

*

Nepotism exists among squirrels. When Beldings squirrels spot coyotes or other predators threatening their community, they don't always whistle a warning. By whistling they risk drawing attention to themselves, so they only raise the alarm if the squirrels that are threatened are members of their family. Otherwise they will leave the squirrels to perish.

*

Fish find power as much of a turn-on as humans do. Studies have found that males who win dominant positions within fish communities are less stressed. They also grow heavier sexual organs and have more sex-related activity in their brains.

*

Moving up the social ladder can make anyone swell up with pride, but a species of African fish gets particularly bigheaded. The chichlid lives in a strictly hierarchical society in which a male's status depends on whether or not it is reproducing. If it makes the step from subordinate to dominant male, the male chichlid immediately changes from a dull gray color to the bright blue or yellow of a senior fish. The fish's testes also grow. But the most remarkable effect is on the chichlid's brain. Cells there swell to eight times their previous size.

Codfathers:
How Animals Behave Like the Mafia

Dolphins carry out kidnappings and form warring gangs. Male bottle-nosed dolphins form small gangs, normally of three members, with a loyalty as fierce as that between mother and children. They stay together for as long as twelve years. The gang's main purpose is to kidnap females with whom they can all have sex. But they do face challenges from other gangs. When this happens, rather like Mafia families, different gangs can form allegiances with each other. "Supergangs" of fourteen dolphins have been observed.

*

Lobsters are mobsters. Becoming the dominant alpha male in his community is every lobster's obsession, and the crustaceans fight constantly to achieve this role. And

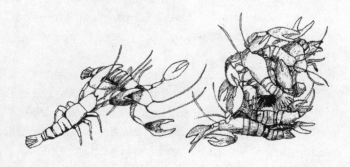

once a lobster has achieved this status he has to keep it. So each night he reminds all the other lobsters in his community who's the boss by throwing them out of their homes and beating them up. Females are strangely attracted to the alpha male's brutality. After being beaten up they visit his home.

*

Emperor penguins stage kidnappings.

In one study more than half of the chicks thought to have been adopted had in fact been stolen from their real parents.

*

Crime pays, for some creatures. Female roseate terns steal fish from the mouths of other birds, sometimes in midflight. Studies revealed that the mothers' midair muggings improved the quality of their offspring in comparison to the hatchlings of birds who led a more honest life.

*

Being a big fish in a small pond can turn a trout into a bully. Medium-sized fish who spent time with violent bigger fish took it out on smaller fish afterwards, demonstrating what psychologists call "displaced aggression."

*

Some female fish can be so spiteful and malicious they drive others to early graves. Females from the threespine species of stickleback steal and eat eggs from nests looked after by their males. They do this even though they are harming their own species and could just as easily steal eggs from a close relative, the blackspotted stickleback.

The females' dastardly behavior makes the male threespine sticklebacks extremely stressed. Males living in fear of the female tend to lose weight and die sooner, even if they are not directly attacked by one. Often simply the sight, sound, and smell of the female is enough to make the male die of nerves.

*

Woodpeckers can behave like thugs. No woodpecker behaves worse than the pileated woodpecker that preys on another, smaller species, the red-cockaded woodpecker. The red-cockaded bird spends up to six years excavating and perfecting the cavity in the ground that is its nest. But when the pileated woodpecker discovers the nest it destroys it in an afternoon.

*

Penguins are racist. Albino penguins are routinely pecked at and shunned by their peers.

It's a Woman's World:
How the "Weaker" Sex Runs
the Ultimate Matriarchal Societies

Sexual equality, at least in terms of size, is commonplace among mammals. But this isn't the case elsewhere in the animal world where females are generally much larger in size. Here, animals live in the ultimate matriarchal societies.

The female blanket octopus, for instance, is 40,000 times heavier than the male. The jelly-bean-sized male is only as big as the pupil in the female's eye. One scientist compared the blanket octopi's mating process as a sparrow trying to have sex with a fighter jet.

*

Perhaps the most mismatched couple of all are the male and female of the green spoon worm. The female is 200,000 times the size of the male. This, predictably, leaves the male very much in his partner's shadow. He spends his entire life perched inside a special chamber within her body doing nothing but fertilizing her eggs. Scientists have named the chamber the androccium—literally, the "small man room."

*

It's a woman's world for wasps, too. In the female-dominated colonies of the paper wasp, the male's only role is to mate with the queen. Once it has fulfilled this role, it is considered a drain on resources and is held prisoner in a cell, where it is repeatedly stung and denied access to the colony's food supplies.

*

In the world of the spotted hyena, females are absolute rulers.

Bigger than males, they have complete control of when and with whom they mate because it is physically impossible for a male to force himself on a female without her permission. (Their sexual supremacy is also connected to the fact they have one of the strangest of all sexual organs—an enlarged, erect clitoris that looks like a penis.) As a result, female hyenas choose men who have got to know them over time and are friendly ahead of those who are aggressive and try to impose themselves.

A hyena community also operates according to a

tightly structured hierarchy, again with men at the bottom of the pile. Those at the top get first access to food, for instance. Females ensure their status is continued through the generations by passing their rank down from mother to daughter.

*

Scientists have discovered the ultimate feminist society, a breed of spider mites that is made up entirely of females. There are other species that have no use for males, including various insects, lizards, snakes, and fish, who can all lay unfertilized eggs that contain copies of their own genes. (No mammals have made men redundant—yet.) The "false spider mite" is unique even among these, however, in that unlike other self-sufficient female species, it doesn't reproduce males.

PART EIGHT

NOT-SO-DUMB ANIMALS: WHY CREATURES ARE MORE INTELLIGENT THAN YOU THINK

How they ever earned the adjective "dumb" is quite a puzzle. Animals display levels of cunning, creativity, and logic to compete with those of humans. Creatures are capable of counting and calculating angles, remembering complex directions, and recognizing songs. Here are some of the mind-boggling things animals achieve when they use their brains.

Two Bees or Not Two Bees?
Animals That Can Put Two
and Two Together

A variety of animals know the difference between more and less, suggesting they can count. In a standard test, human children, given the choice between a jar with two cookies and a jar with three, will go for the jar with the most cookies. In a similar way, monkeys go for containers with three apples rather than those with two, and salamanders go for test tubes with three insects.

*

Monkeys have demonstrated they can put quantities of objects, ranging from 1 to 9 in number, in ascending order. This suggests they have basic counting skills.

*

Honeybees can count, too.

*

Parrots have shown they may understand the concept of zero—an idea children usually don't grasp until they are four years old.

*

Bumblebees can solve complex color puzzles. In a laboratory experiment, scientists set honey-seeking bees a multiple-choice exam in which they had to pick out different colored flowers whose hues changed against different colored lights. The bees passed the exam with, ah, flying colors.

*

Animals understand that a bird in the hand is worth two in the bush. A study showed that tufted capuchin monkeys were more worried about losing wealth than gaining it, demonstrating a human trait scientists call "loss aversion."

*

Fiddler crabs are excellent at trigonometry. The mud-flat-dwelling crabs are always on the lookout for rivals ready to steal their burrows. When they spot a potential thief, they combine visual information on the crab's location with the additional data provided by a built in "odometer," that measures by smell how far they have wandered from home. The crabs use these two pieces of information to triangulate the intruder's position in relation to them and their burrow. This tells them how great the threat is and they act accordingly.

*

Ants never encounter traffic jams. They have the ability to ferry food back and forth to their nests at the same speed regardless of whether they have a wide or narrow route to travel. Even bottlenecks of ants heading in opposite directions don't slow them down. They have a system of moving past each other in groups that keeps things moving at the same speed.

*

Seals can understand whale conversations. Harbor seals eavesdrop on the underwater chatter so as to distinguish whether approaching whales are fish eaters or those that prey on seals and dolphins.

*

Rats can learn the difference between languages. In an experiment, Spanish scientists discovered that the rodents could distinguish between Dutch and Japanese.

*

If you pay peanuts, you get monkeys, or so the old phrase goes. But even capuchin monkeys will protest if they aren't paid a fair wage. In experiments, the monkeys refused rewards for doing tasks when they knew other monkeys had been paid better. The tests suggest they too have a sense of fairness.

I Remember Ewe:
Why Elephants Aren't the Only Animals
Who Don't Forget

Sheep are good at remembering faces. In an experiment, some sheep were able to recognize the faces of 50 sheep and 10 humans. They were also able to remember them for two years.

Sheep are also able to tell the difference between various human expressions. They prefer smiling faces to angry ones. Female sheep are more attracted to the faces of older males.

*

Gorillas, chimpanzees, and other apes recognize themselves in mirrors. Monkeys don't, although they do realize their reflections are not living creatures.

*

Fish have much better memories than is commonly thought. Australian freshwater rainbowfish were able to remember an escape route eleven months after they first discovered it. Given the fish only live for two to three years, that is the equivalent of a human recalling something twenty to thirty years later.

*

The octopus is a quick learner. In one study a group of octopi were left to watch another group performing a simple exercise in which they had to select one of two balls. Selecting one produced a reward, while picking the other brought mild punishment. When the observers were then asked to repeat the exercise they did so making very few mistakes.

*

Cats have better memories than dogs. Tests conducted by the University of Michigan concluded that while a dog's memory lasts no more than five minutes, a cat's can last as long as sixteen hours—exceeding even that of monkeys and orangutans.

*

Border collies are capable of understanding language so that they can perform tasks as well as three-year-old humans. A dog called Rico was asked to choose two toys from a choice of ten on twenty occasions. Each toy was given a unique word. Rico correctly fetched 37 of the 40 toys he was asked to collect. He successfully completed the task a month later, correctly getting 50 percent of the toys.

THE TEN BRIGHTEST BREEDS OF DOG
   (Ranked according to the ability to understand new commands in less than five repetitions and the ability to obey
   first commands 95 percent of the time or better.)

   1. Border collie
   2. Poodle

3. German shepherd
4. Golden retriever
5. Doberman pinscher
6. Shetland sheepdog
7. Labrador retriever
8. Papillon
9. Rottweiler
10. Australian cattle dog

THE ELEVEN LEAST BRIGHT BREEDS OF DOG
(Ranked, with most intelligent first, according to the ability to understand new commands, even after hundreds of repetitions.)

1. Shih tzu
2. Basset hound
3. Mastiff
4. Beagle
5. Pekingese
6. Bloodhound
7. Borzoi
8. Chow chow
9. Bulldog
10. Basenji
11. Afghan hound

Small parasitic wasps can be trained to sniff out drugs and explosives. Unlike dogs, which take years to be readied for the job, the wasps learn the task in half an hour.

*

Monkeys have displayed an ability to remember children's songs. "Happy Birthday," "Old MacDonald Had a Farm," and "Row, Row, Row Your Boat" were among those they recognized when the songs were played back to them.

*

Scrub jaybirds have particularly good memories. They can remember not only where they hide food but also what kind of food it is, studies have revealed.

*

Elephants really don't forget, at least grandmother elephants don't and their descendants are grateful for it. Research has shown that herds of elephants draw on the wisdom and experience of elder females. The elderly elephants use their own memories to show the younger herd members how to respond to threats and strangers.

These female elders choose where the herd eats and drinks and which young members are kept in the group or expelled. Families with grandmother elephants are less stressed and produce more offspring.

*

Seals never forget their mothers.

Studies of northern fur seals have found that mothers and their children remember each other's calls long after they have been separated. Unusual for mammals, the seals recognized and responded to each other's voices as long as four years after they went their separate ways.

*

Honeybees can recognize human faces. In an experiment, bees correctly identified different faces more than 80 percent of the time.

*

And finally a word of warning to those who think exercise helps improve the mental processes . . .

Too much running on a wheel makes mice stupid. Tests have shown that hyperactive mice who run compulsively around and around on wheels and elsewhere are slower learners.

Knock, Knock, Who's Bear?
The Cunning (and Criminal) Workings
of the Animal Mind

Bears can trick people into letting them into homes by knocking on their doors. A bear in Croatia pulled off the trick three times at the same house. Each time the bear calmly walked into the house and helped itself to the contents of the kitchen.

*

Wallabies know that one good turn deserves another.

In 1996, an Australian farmer was awakened in the middle of the night by a deafening thumping on his bedroom door. It was the wallaby he had taken in and cared for after it had been hit and injured by a car. The wallaby was alerting the farmer that his house was on fire.

*

Tiny Spanish fly beetles have a cunning way of conning their way into the affections of much larger male bees. Hundreds of the tiny, young blister beetles cluster together in lumps that they form to look like female bees. The hapless male bees fall for the trick then offer their new "girlfriends" a lift into their nests.

*

A Malaysian ant that makes its home inside a giant bamboo has come up with a clever way of coping with rising tides. If the bamboo becomes flooded, the ant drinks as much water as it can, then runs outside to pee. It then returns to start the process all over again.

*

Cats may be able to dial 911. Police responding to an emergency call to the home of a man called Gary Rosheisen found him lying paralyzed on the floor having fallen out of his wheelchair. Mr. Rosheisen couldn't have used either of the special alarms in his house, one above his bed and the other on a necklace, which he had forgotten to wear that day. The police did, however, find his ginger cat, Tommy, lying by the telephone.

*

The term "birdbrained" is misleading. Jays deliberately sit on ant nests to anger the inhabitants. The ants exit to soak the bird with formic acid. This is precisely what the jay wants. The formic acid is a natural pesticide and rids it of many of the main parasites that feed on it.

*

Carrion crows living in cities take food they can't crack open to roadsides. They place hard-shelled snacks like nuts and clams so they can be run over by a passing car, bus, or truck, then retrieve it. To minimize the risk of getting hit by a speeding car the crows often do their nut- and clam-cracking at pedestrian crossings with traffic lights. They wait for the red lights before placing and collecting their food.

*

Some birds in the rain forest have worked out how to sing to the gallery. The leafy canopy of the rain forest has acoustics which make longer notes resonate louder, as they would in a concert hall. To make sure their song is heard, birds like the Venezuelan white-necked thrush produce elongated notes that in turn produce much higher decibel levels than other species'.

*

Herons are canny fly fishermen. Greenbacked herons have been observed dropping a range of baits—from seeds and flowers to feathers and dead flies—on to the surface of rivers and lakes. The birds then stand by motionless until they get a bite.

*

Killer whales quickly learn the tricks of their trade.

A study of the ingenious predator at a marine park observed how a four-year-old male cleverly lured gulls to their deaths by regurgitating fish and spitting it onto the surface of the water. When the gulls reached for the fish, the whale captured them in its jaws.

Within weeks the whale's younger half brother was repeating the trick, previously unseen at the park. Researchers concluded the young whale could only have learned it from his older sibling.

*

The cuckoo is one of the great con artists of the animal world. It can trick other birds into raising its children by laying their eggs in the stranger's nest. When the cuckoo chicks hatch, the youngsters continue their parents' strategy by killing any other birds in the nest before they reveal their identity. Scientists have found the imposter cuckoo even fools the foster parent into thinking its chicks are still alive by flapping yellow patches on its wings. This also creates the illusion there are more mouths to feed and tricks the foster parent into delivering more food.

Scientists think cuckoos are able to fool other birds by producing eggs that, while looking mismatched to the human eye, seem fine to the hosts because they see them in the ultraviolet spectrum.

One bird the cuckoo may find immune to its tricks, however, is the American coot. The coot also lays eggs in neighbors' nests, and, wary of having the same thing done to them, has developed countermeasures. To be sure which chicks are theirs—and which chicks are not—the coots have learned to count.

*

Fish can fool birds into feeding them.

In a study, a goldfish learned that simply by emerging from the water and opening its mouth it could persuade a cardinal bird to feed it insects. Scientists think the bird mistook the goldfish's mouth for that of a hungry hatchling. The fish continued to obtain food in this way for several weeks.

*

Male insects get away with giving their partners fake presents. It is common for the males to give their female partners presents, perhaps food, a drop of saliva, or part of a dried insect. These are usually eaten during sex. But scientists have discovered that some insects give presents like seeds that, while looking good, have no useful purpose. The females still accept them and have sex.

*

Orangutans can commit jailbreaks.

Two apes famously collaborated to break out of London Zoo. Together they improvised a tool which they used to pry open the wires of the zoo's ape house. The apes were recaptured, but one of them repeated the escape act soon afterwards. It broke free by throwing a flowerpot through the window protecting his cage.

*

Turtles do a tap dance to draw worms from the earth.

Wood turtles in Pennsylvania were observed stomping the earth in a rhythmic pattern, first with one front foot, then with the other. The one-beat-per-second dance regularly drew earthworms from the ground. The moment they appeared the turtle snapped them up. In studies, turtles successfully lured an average of 2.4 worms per hour. The most skilled tap dancer, however, caught 7 worms in just eight minutes.

*

Leopards store their carrion high in trees to avoid having it stolen by lions and hyenas.

*

The sting of the deadly fire ant is so fierce it kills most creatures. However, the Brazilian Orasema wasp has learned to mimic the smell of the fire ant so well that it is able to penetrate its nest without being attacked. Once there it eats the ants' larvae.

*

The aye-aye, a species of lemur from Madagascar, has a unique technique for finding food. The aye-aye feeds off grubs that live in cavities underground, mainly in the roots of trees. Its senses are so sharp it can not only locate these cavities by tapping on the trunk of a tree but also tell whether the cavities are empty or not.

*

An Australian spider lures its prey by covering its web with scented bait. The pleasant smell of rotting plants draws in unsuspecting insects.

*

It takes a thief to know a thief. Scrub jays with a criminal record take great care to hide their own stores of food from birds who might give them a taste of their own medicine.

*

Some wasps have a clever way of getting access to ants' nests. The wasps can secrete a cocktail of chemicals that make the ants start fighting with each other. While the mass brawl is going on, the wasp sneaks in and helps itself to a meal.

*

Ravens can plant red herrings. The birds are highly competitive over food. Ravens have been seen leading other birds to believe there is food in a particular spot, then sneaking off to where there really is food while the others stage a vain search for scraps.

*

Brainy monkeys are the sneakiest. The most likely to deceive their peers are gorillas, chimpanzees, bonobos, orangutans, and macaque monkeys, who have the largest neocortex area of their brain relative to their size. The most trustworthy are bush babies and lemurs.

PART NINE

BASIC INSTINCTS:
EXTRAORDINARY ANIMAL POWERS

Animals are equipped with a range of high-tech gadgetry that would put the CIA to shame. They see, hear, smell, taste, and feel their way around their world using everything from hair-trigger antennae and sonar to stereophonic smell detectors and rotating ears. Some species are even equipped with what, to us at least, seem like sixth senses. The most extraordinary animals can spot earthquakes and smell cancer, they can see colors in the dark and cure themselves from disease.

Hear All Evil:
How Animals See, Smell, Hear,
and Echolocate

A chameleon has eyes that can move independently of each other, thus allowing it to see in two different directions at the same time. The sea horse has a similar ability. The pigeon has its eyes mounted laterally on its head so that it can see for an impressive 340 degrees around it, everywhere in fact, except the back of its head.

Perhaps the most impressive eyesight of all is possessed by predatory birds. Buzzards can spot small rodents while flying at a height of 15,000 feet. While humans have 20/20 vision, hawks have 20/5 vision. This means the details we can see from 5 feet away the hawk can see from a distance of 20 feet.

Dogs can see a moving object up to 985 yards away. They can see a static object up to 640 yards away.

The eyesight of spiders varies widely from species to species. Most spiders have eight eyes, some have up to a dozen. But some also have none at all. Even if they do have a full set of eyes, most spiders can only tell the difference between light and dark.

*

Box jellyfish have twenty-four eyes and four brains. They also have sixty anuses.

*

An ostrich's eye is bigger than its brain.

*

Octopi have brains in their legs.

Studies have shown the octopus can delegate some thought processes from its central brain to smart nerves in its tentacles.

*

The housefly tastes with its feet, which are 10 million times more sensitive than a human tongue.

*

Giraffes have a highly flexible and versatile tongue. They use it, amongst other things, for cleaning out their ears.

*

Fruit flies breathe through their tongues, which they use to pump oxygen into their bodies.

*

Ants can hear with their knees. They pick up vibrations both in their nests and when on overgrowth on the ground.

*

The golden frog, a rare amphibian from Costa Rica and Panama, has no working ear. Instead it hears through its skin, which is tuned to vibrate to the same frequency as frog voices.

*

Cats have ears that can rotate rapidly to identify sound and are so highly tuned they can hear frequencies up to 64,000

Hz. (A human can hear up to around 23,000 Hz.) This means they can even hear the ultrasonic sounds made by rodents. This is why they can sometimes locate and pounce on a mouse without actually seeing it in advance.

*

Cats can hear 10 octaves. Humans can hear only 8.5.

*

Using their swiveling ears like radar dishes, dogs can locate the source of a sound in 6/100ths of a second. They can hear sounds 250 yards away that a human would only be able to hear at 25 yards. They can also pick up on frequencies of up to 45,000 Hz.

*

Fruit flies have a rotating ear that also acts as a nose. Zebras can rotate their ears to detect sound without moving their bodies.

*

Geckos and moths can see colors in the dark.

*

Far from being "as blind as bats," the world's most common flying mammal is equipped with an array of sensory devices that are second to none.

To find their way around, bats use a system known as echolocation in which they bounce sound waves off objects and other creatures that cross their paths. A bat can not only detect potential prey like insects as far as 18 feet away, but can also work out what kind of creature it is. Using their nose leaf they can also pick up the warmth of an animal from about six inches away.

Dolphins also use echolocation.

*

Catfish have night vision. They can track prey, such as guppy, in pitch-black waters by following the chemical traces in the other fish's wake.

*

Birds look at objects with one eye only, probably because they use their left and right eyes for different functions. The left eye is better suited to picking up colors while the right eye is more tuned to detecting movements.

*

Lizards navigate by using a third eye on top of their heads.

*

Sharks can pick up even the dimmest sources of light underwater. They can detect a glow that is 10 times dimmer than anything the human eye is capable of seeing.

*

Sharks also have a phenomenal sense of smell. A white-tip shark put in a tank that had just been emptied of an injured fish duplicated every move the fish had made, tracing exactly the same zigzag patterns.

The tiniest whiff of an injured or dead fish will send a shark into a feeding frenzy. If their prey is alive, the more stress it displays, the more excited the shark gets.

*

Rats smell in stereo. Their two nostrils work independently of each other to sniff out odors. They then report back to the brain, which works out what they are picking up. This gives them a big advantage over prey and potential predators.

*

Most mammals, including humans and mice, lose the hair inside their ears as they get older, leading to deafness. Bats are the only known exception to this. They can regenerate the cells within their ears and grow new hair.

*

A dog's sense of smell is 100,000 times better than a human's. In tests dogs have been able to pick up chemical solutions that form 1 or 2 parts per trillion. That is the equivalent of smelling one bad apple in two billion barrels.

*

The male cotton leaf worm may have the most sensitive sense of smell in all of the animal world. It can smell the sex pheromone of its female if there are just five molecules of it in about half a cubic inch of air. The Swedish scientist who measured this compared it to a human sensing a sugar cube had been dropped in a lake by taking one sip of its water.

*

Alligators and crocodiles don't rely on their normal senses to detect potential prey in the water. The reptiles are equipped with a sophisticated sensory system they inherited from their dinosaur ancestors. The hair-trigger sensors, or receptors, are dotted around the jaws of alligators and the faces and bodies of crocodiles. They are so sensitive they can pick up on a deer sipping from the water many yards away.

*

Crickets have supersensitive hairs that can warn them of predators creeping up on them. The hairs, or cerci, are so finely tuned they can detect even the tiniest change in the air current caused by the wings of a wasp or the tongue of a toad.

*

A cat's whiskers, or vibrissae, are among the most sophisticated radar devices in the animal world. These supersensitive instruments act as feelers and allow the cat to determine if a space is too small to squeeze through. They can also help detect the movement of prey. Cats have these whiskers on the back of their forelegs as well as on their faces.

*

If you shave a bat's wings it will lose its power to navigate safely in the dark. The underside of the wings are equipped with tiny, hairlike touch receptors that help it detect turbulence. A scientist treated these receptors with a depilatory cream and watched what happened. When the guinea pig bats needed to make 90-degree turns to avoid objects, they couldn't control their vertical elevation. Some bats hit the ceiling. The bats were able to fly safely again only when the hairs grew back.

*

Breathing can be dangerous for some insects. Butterflies and ants have such fragile bodies that if they breathed all the time there would be such a buildup of oxygen it would kill them. As a result they adjust their breathing to control their intake of oxygen when resting.

Southpaws:
How Some Animals Lead
with Their Left

Female horses put their right foot first, males step forward with their left.

In a study of untrained horses in Ireland, researchers watched which leg they stepped forward with, in which direction they moved to avoid an obstacle, and on which side they rolled over when lying down in a bed of hay.

Surprisingly, most female horses favored their right side, while most males did things with their left side. Only one in ten of the horses alternated between left and right.

*

Walruses are right-flippered. In a study of walruses digging for clams in waters off Greenland, researchers found they used their right flipper 89 percent of the time.

*

Marmosets are more likely to be left-handed. Most crows are right-handed as are the majority of humpback whales. (Most whales have five fingers in their flippers.)

*

Rats that forage for food using their right whiskers are more successful than those who use their left whiskers.

*

Eight out of ten chimpanzees and gorillas cradle their babies against the left side of their body. (The ratio is similar in human mothers.)

*

Deadly cane toads are more likely to attack other animals if they are on the left rather than the right.

*

West is best, at least for aardvarks. The anteaters forage for food in the evenings when termites have gathered inside their mounds. The termites can't generate their own heat and are drawn to the western side of the nest by the warmth of the setting sun. Rather than attacking it randomly, one in two anteaters tackles the west wing of the termite mound first.

Animal Doctors:
How Creatures Can Heal Themselves
(and Others)

Scientists have found that animals are capable of treating themselves medically. When pregnant elephants in East Africa are ready to give birth, for instance, they make a special journey to eat a small tree, the boraginaceae. One study observed a heavily pregnant female march around 17 miles to find and eat the tree, which didn't grow in her normal habitat. Afterwards she returned home and gave birth within days. Local women who want to induce labor use the same method.

*

Chimpanzees have been observed curing themselves of bad cases of stomach sickness. A chimpanzee suffering from diarrhea and general malaise was seen making its way to a small tree from which it peeled away a piece of bark. She then began chewing on the bark for half an hour, spitting out the fibers as she did so. Within twenty-four hours she was completely recovered.

*

Brazilian monkeys use their own equivalent of contraceptives.

The female muriqui monkeys eat the leaves of a plant which contains ingredients called isoflavanoids, similar to estrogen. Scientists think they may take this to decrease their fertility. When they are ready to breed, however, they chew on another leaf which contains a pregnancy hormone called stigmasterol.

*

Many animals take herbal remedies.

Wild boars and Indian elephants eat plant roots to keep parasitic worms at bay. Bears eat a plant from the family *ligusticum*. They chew it up, then spit it out mashed up with saliva. They then methodically smear it on their paws and fur. Scientists think the lotion acts as an insecticide and prevents parasites.

*

Ants produce antibiotics to control diseases in their colonies.

*

Chimpanzees prevent illness by chewing the leaves of particular plants. Humans who have tried the leaves of these plants have discovered they have the same pharmacological properties as prescription drugs. Scientists believe leaf chewing has other purposes within the ape world. Female howler monkeys use them to influence the sex of their children, while some monkeys may take them as recreational drugs.

*

Sparrows know how to protect themselves from disease. When an outbreak of malaria hit Calcutta, India, the sparrows started lining their nest with leaves from the krish-nachura tree. They then ate the leaves containing quinine, which kills the malaria parasite.

*

Dogs can apparently smell cancer. Clinical tests, vetted by the University of California, Berkeley, have shown that simply by sniffing samples of human's breath, dogs can detect lung, breast, and other cancers with an accuracy rate of between 88 percent and 97 percent. The accuracy rate of a multimillion-dollar hospital scanner is between 85 percent and 90 percent.

Dogs can also be trained to alert people with heart conditions they are about to suffer an attack.

*

Some dogs can also predict in advance when a child is about to have an epileptic seizure. A Canadian study found that dogs who lived with children prone to epileptic episodes behaved unusually in advance of the attacks.

Some dogs would lick the child's face or act protectively. One dog even guided a young girl away from a flight of stairs shortly before she had an attack. The dogs' warnings came as early as five hours before the first symptoms of the epileptic episode were visible.

*

Numerous scientific studies have proven that having dogs or cats around significantly lowers stress and blood pressure levels.

*

Donkeys have a soothing effect on other animals.

Passive creatures by nature, they calm other species that are nervous or recovering from injury. They are also used routinely as companions for humans suffering from mental and physical disabilities. No one has satisfactorily explained why they have this influence on other species.

*

Modern doctors are returning to the ancient practice of using maggots as specialist "microsurgeons." Maggots, in particular species of fly larvae like blowflies, have the ability to treat human tissue damaged by such conditions as foot and leg ulcers, burns, and postoperative wounds. Between 5 and 10 of them are placed on each square centimeter (about one-sixth of an inch) of a wound, which is then wrapped in dressing and left for between 48 and 72 hours. In that time, the maggots dissolve the dead tissue by secreting digestive juices and then ingesting the liquefied tissue and any bacteria. The maggots grow five times their original size during the process.

*

Some of the animal world's deadliest animals may also have the ability to cure humans. The powerful venom of tropical cone snails is thought to have the potential to cure a range of illnesses, from cancer to epilepsy. Some snake venoms are believed to be, potentially, a source for even more cures. A new type of drug, ACE inhibitors, used to treat high blood pressure and other cardiovascular disorders, has been developed from the venom of a Brazilian snake, for instance. Other snake venoms are seen as potential agents for preventing the growth of cancerous tumors.

*

A chemical extracted from the skin of an Ecuadorian frog produces a painkiller 200 times more powerful than morphine.

Unearthly Powers:
How Animals Use Their Sixth Sense

The idea that animals can predict earthquakes has gained some acceptance by scientists.

A U.S. study found that 17 out of 50 homes near the scene of a Californian quake in 1977 reported odd behavior in their animals. This ranged from a horse kicking the sides of its stall to a cat pacing around and fidgeting during its normal nap time and a normally placid dog whining excitedly. Studies in the Mojave desert in the United States also found that dogs barked at small aftershocks unnoticed by humans but picked up by seismometers.

*

Some animals go into a strange, drunken state before earthquakes.

In the weeks leading up to the catastrophic earthquake that hit the Chinese city of Haicheng in 1975, people reported seeing dazed-looking rats and snakes that appeared to be frozen in place. In the days immediately before the quake hit, animals became increasingly restless, with cows and horses in an agitated state, chickens refusing to stay in their coops, and ducks taking to the air much more frequently than normal.

*

New evidence that animals are more closely attuned to the earth's vibrations than humans emerged before the Asian tsunami struck on December 26, 2004. Eyewitnesses reported that elephants screamed and ran for high ground, flamingos abandoned their normal, low-lying breeding grounds, zoo animals cowered away in their cages refusing to come out, and domestic dogs refused to go for their daily walks near the sea. While the human loss of life was horrendous, very few animals perished.

*

Sharks can tell when a hurricane is brewing.

Just before Tropical Storm Gabrielle hit southwestern Florida in 2001, for instance, every member of a group of blacktip sharks being tracked with radio tags placed by biologists fled their normal habitat and swam to deeper waters. Similarly, before that year's Hurricane Charley hit, another group of tagged sharks made a break for deeper waters. Marine biologists think sharks can sense the drop in atmospheric pressure that occurs as a hurricane moves in. The drop in air pressure produces a similar drop in water pressure.

*

Dogs can sense mortar or artillery fire.

A study of dog behavior during the siege of Sarajevo discovered many dogs behaved oddly in advance of the beginning of shelling. Around 57 percent of dogs tucked their heads under tables or other items of furniture. Thirty-five percent of dogs hid their entire bodies by crawling under a bed or table. Around 14 percent of dogs jumped into their owners' arms while 21 percent whined as if to warn of the oncoming fire. The most intriguing discovery, however, concerned dogs that were out walking with their owners when the gunfire was about to start. Almost 72 percent of them physically dragged their owners somewhere else. In many instances, the study found, the dogs successfully moved their owners from the artillery's firing line.

*

Animals can levitate. Placed in a powerful electromagnetic field, creatures from frogs to grizzly bear cubs have hovered in midair.

PART TEN

DO THE LOCOMOTION:
HOW ANIMALS GET FROM A TO B

Some slither, some fly, some bounce, some simply hitch a ride—all animals need to keep on the move, but some are better and more adventurous travelers than others.

Nature's greatest explorers are equipped with the equivalent of compasses and GPS systems and can circumnavigate the globe with seeming ease. The animal kingdom's less athletic creatures, on the other hand, are barely capable of putting one foot in front of the other.

Poetry in Motion:
Nature's Greatest Movers

The kangaroo is one of the natural world's most efficient running machines. A kangaroo's stride when it is in full flight and running at more than 20 miles per hour can be more than 20 feet long. Yet the faster it hops, the less energy it uses. Scientists think the kangaroo's legs and tail, which work in tandem, operate in the same, energy-efficient way as the mechanism of a pogo stick.

The kangaroo is also the only mammal that stops sweating the moment it stops exercising. Instead it starts panting furiously at the rate of 300 times a minute, allowing it to cool down its overheated body without losing too much water.

*

Dolphins are among nature's most efficient and ingenious swimmers.

They can sustain speeds of more than 20 miles per hour by swimming along at a depth of between 5 and 10 feet, then leaping out of the water when they get closer to the surface. They leap out not for fun but to conserve energy. It is easier to move through the air than through the water where, at that depth, their bodies create waves. The so-called spinner dolphin has taken this a stage further. It emerges from the water liked a coiled spring to perform up to seven corkscrew rolls in the air. Dolphins can also surf, spending up to an hour riding the bow wave at the head of a ship without expending any energy or moving their bodies.

*

The deepest dive recorded is 2,099.74 feet by a leatherback turtle. It is believed the turtle is capable of diving even further, down to 3,281 feet.

*

The world's largest rodent, the capybara, is a talented diver. It can remain underwater for up to 5 minutes.

*

Emperor penguins can dive to a depth of 1,500 feet and hold their breath for up to 22 minutes.

*

Squid and octopi are equipped with jet engines.

They suck water in through a wide opening in their bodies, then launch themselves by firing it back out through a funnel-like organ. The funnel is movable to allow movement in different directions.

*

The plumed basilisk, a Central American lizard, has a unique ability. When threatened, it can run across the

surface of still water on its hind feet at speeds of 6.5 feet per second. The lizard does this by creating pockets of air under its feet. The trick has earned it a predictable nickname: the Jesus Christ lizard.

*

Snails and slugs produce a colorless, sticky mucus discharge that forms a protective carpet under them as they travel along. The discharge is so effective that they can crawl over rough and even knife-sharp surfaces. They also use the discharge for navigation. A snail's trail has breaks in it. A slug's is continuous.

*

Geckos are the natural world's stickiest creatures. A gecko can race up a polished glass wall at a speed of 3.3 feet per second and can support its entire body weight while hanging from a wall by a single toe. It can do this because it has tiny sticky pads on its feet, called spatulae. Many creatures have these, but few have as many as the gecko. Flies have thousands of spatulae, geckos have millions.

*

The greater glider, a tree-dwelling marsupial from Australasia, has perhaps the most superpowered senses of any animal. Its stereoscopic vision and stereophonic hearing allow it to parachute horizontal distances of more than 328 feet to land on the tiniest of branches. And all this is done at night.

*

The most unusual airborne creatures are probably flying snakes. While almost every other flying creature—even flying squirrels—use some form of symmetrically paired wings, the paradise tree snake, one of three types of flyers from southeast Asia, has its own unique aerodynamic technique. As it flies through the treetops, the snake flattens its body and effectively slithers through the air.

*

The highest altitude at which a bird has been recorded flying is 37,000 feet. This is 2,000 feet higher than the normal cruising height of a commercial airliner.

*

The whipnose anglerfish is thought to be unique. It is the only fish to have been filmed swimming upside down. It adopts the pose when trawling the depths of the ocean for prey.

*

Electric fish can swim backwards as easily as they can forwards.

*

Hummingbirds are the only birds that can fly backwards.

*

Dragonflies are the fastest insects and have been known to travel at 35 miles an hour. Hawk moths, which have been clocked at a speed of 33.7 miles per hour, are believed to be the second-fastest insects.

*

The fastest creatures on earth, according to the Smithsonian National Zoological Park in Washington, D.C., are:

Fastest mammal on land: cheetah, maximum speed 70 miles per hour

Fastest mammal in water: Dall porpoise, maximum speed 35 miles per hour

Fastest bird in the air: peregrine falcon, maximum diving speed 200 miles per hour

Fastest bird on land: North African ostrich, maximum speed 45 miles per hour

Fastest fish: sailfish, maximum speed 68 miles per hour

The cheetah can accelerate from 0 to 45 miles per hour in 2.5 seconds.

Globe-Trotters:
Long-Distance Animals

The northern elephant seal travels farther than any known mammal. Each year it commutes twice from the feeding grounds of the Pacific or California coast to travel all the way towards Alaska and the north Pacific for the breeding season. The seal covers around 12,427 miles in all.

*

The male albatross can spend thirty-three days out at sea foraging for food on the southern oceans.

*

You could call it traveling light. Migrating birds ensure they cover huge distances by destroying their internal organs. A bird called the bar-tailed godwit, which flies 6,835 miles from its breeding ground in Alaska to New Zealand, gets rid of most of its gut, kidneys, and liver to be able to carry the extra food needed for the journey. The godwit rebuilds the organs when it reaches journey's end.

*

The screw-worm fly is one of the animal kingdom's most prodigious—and dangerous—travelers. The fly's maggots attack livestock, causing huge damage. Having been eradicated from America, it transferred to the rest of the world by getting itself onto passenger planes and ships.

*

Snails are among nature's most successful hitchhikers. European snails have been discovered on the remote Atlantic island of Tristan da Cunha, 5,592 miles from their roots. Cambridge scientists think they got there by hitching a ride on migrating birds.

*

Iguanas have used rafts to travel around the Caribbean. Scientists think they hitch a lift on pieces of debris thrown up during storms to travel more than 200 miles between islands.

*

Cold-water fish may have a secret pathway that mysteriously allows them to travel from pole to pole. Fish from the icy southern oceans have been found in the equally cold waters of the far north, despite the fact they would have had to swim through the tropics to get there. A toothfish from Patagonia, a native of the waters off Antarctica, was found off the west coast of Greenland. Scientists believe there may be a deep-water corridor of freezing water that leads fish from one end of the planet to the other.

*

Monarch butterflies have built-in magnetic compasses. Each autumn the butterflies make one of the most remarkable journeys in the animal world, fluttering 2,500 miles from their breeding grounds in the eastern United States and Canada to their winter retreat in Mexico. Millions of them get to Mexico safely despite never having been to their home there before. Scientists believe they use a combination of the sun and magnetic fields to guide them. Other animals believed to have such compasses include honeybees, wasps, some fish, and a species of mole rat.

*

Many animals are thought to have a similar ability to follow the earth's magnetic fields, but two animals stand out as masters of magnetic orientation. Each year the Arctic tern travels from Antarctica in the south to the Arctic in the north and back, a round-trip journey of 20,000 miles. It does this without ever straying off course.

Equally impressive is the female green turtle, which each year travels from its feeding grounds off the coast of South America to its breeding grounds on the island of Ascension in the middle of the Atlantic. Precisely how the turtle navigates the 1,500 miles of open ocean to locate the 6.8-mile-wide pinprick of rock that is Ascension no one knows.

*

The Californian red-bellied newt has such a phenomenal ability to find its way home, almost as though it has a GPS device inside it. The lizardlike creature's senses are so powerful it can find its way home from miles away. One red-bellied newt was moved from its home in a valley, carried across a mountain divide 984 feet high, and deposited in a new environment. The moment it was placed down it oriented itself, pointed its head towards home, and began its journey back. Scientists believe this compass is linked to a mysterious third chamber in the newt's nose. The chamber doesn't pick out smells in the same way the other two do. Some suspect the toad has a different kind of awareness we don't yet understand.

*

Spiny lobsters also have a remarkable ability to find their way home. Lobsters that were moved as far as 24 miles from their starting point and had no visual clues as to where they were immediately pointed in the right direction and headed back to the precise spot they had left. Scientists think the lobster taps into a kind of magnetic map drawn for it by the earth's magnetic field.

*

The largest swarm of locusts ever assembled is thought to be the one that crossed the Red Sea in 1889. The swarm covered an area of 2,000 square miles and was estimated to weigh 500,000 tons and contain 250 billion individual locusts.

*

Traveling broadens the mind, especially if you are a bird. Migrating birds that travel long distances each year have better memories than those who tend to stay at home. Scientists believe the tricks migrating birds learn in navigating their way around the world expand their mental capacities. Two types of warbler were found to have very different abilities in remembering where food was kept. The migrating garden warbler could remember for a year; the stay-at-home Sardinian warbler forgot where the food was kept after just two weeks.

Are We There Yet?
Some Poor Animal Travelers

The giraffe's telescopic legs mean it has to switch from walking to running mode in one seamless movement. If it tries to trot it will trip up.

This is a fate that is unlikely to befall the sloth. It moves so slowly fungus grows on its feet.

*

Ants won't cross a chalk line, so if you want to stop an army of them in their tracks mark one on the floor. This is only one of several tips Joey Green, an American gardening expert, has come up with for keeping the insect at bay.

Among the other everyday household items Green recommends using are baking soda, peppermint soap, flour, white vinegar, and a range of particular brands. These include Vaseline petroleum jelly, Maxwell House coffee, Johnson's baby powder, and Campbell's tomato soup. Apparently, if you place table legs in four empty cans of the latter, the ants will not be able to climb up the table.

*

Why did the bear cross the road? Probably because it was male. Studies have shown that female grizzly bears are much less likely to cross roads than males.

*

Elderly bees get jet lag if flown overseas. The older bees have a powerful internal rhythm to their day and get confused by the change in environment.

PART ELEVEN

CHILDREN OF THE EVOLUTION: NATURE'S SUCCESSES AND FAILURES

All animals are the product of the vast game of trial and error we call evolution. Each species has faced the challenges presented by its environment and adapted—or not adapted—accordingly. Some of the solutions nature has arrived at are truly miraculous. But, to the human eye, at least, some seem more like works in progress, with serious teething troubles left to be ironed out.

Here, finally, is a collection of Mother Nature's greatest hits—and some of her misses too.

Design Classics:
Mother Nature's Greatest Hits

Deep-sea diving penguins have developed a clever trick for avoiding the "bends." King and Adelie penguins are capable of diving hundreds of feet into the ocean and staying there for minutes, yet they are also able to return to the surface quickly without suffering from the decompression sickness that afflicts human divers. They do this by stopping halfway in their ascent then slowly floating to the surface at an oblique angle that allows their lungs to gradually acclimatize.

*

Ostriches have a simple but brilliantly effective method for cooling their legs down during the hottest part of the day. They urinate on them.

*

Emperor penguins never get wet. Their feathers are flat, oily, and watertight so that no water can penetrate them. Their skin is also protected by an air space between their bodies and their feathers.

*

Spiders can weave webs that are so elastic they can stretch to four times their original length then return to normal without any sagging.

*

Crocodiles can hold their breath underwater for more than an hour.

The carbon dioxide that builds up in their blood is converted into tiny ions of bicarbonate. This stimulates the oxygen-carrying hemoglobin in its red blood cells to release vital oxygen into the crocodile's system.

*

The cancer rate in birds is about half that in mammals.

*

The Arizona striped tree lizard is nature's color-coded thermometer. In the morning, when temperatures are low, the colored patches on the lizard's stomach and throat are green. As the sun rises the patches turn turquoise. When the sun is at its brightest and the temperature at its highest the lizard's patches are a bright cobalt blue.

*

The ultimate heat gauge is the tree cricket. Heat and cold directly affect the rate at which it chirps, so that if you count the number of chirps the cricket makes in 15 seconds and add 39 the sum will be the outside temperature in Fahrenheit. Little wonder then that the tree cricket is also known as the poor man's thermometer.

*

An African desert beetle satisfies its thirst in a unique way— by drinking with its backside. The *Stenocara* beetle has to survive in the world's hottest desert, the Namib in south-west Africa. Its only source of water is the moisture in the morning fog. It collects this by pointing itself backwards into the morning breeze and collecting beads of moisture in its specially ridged backside. The captured mist then dribbles along the ridges of its back into its mandibles.

*

An alligator generates around 2,000 pounds of force when it snaps its jaws closed, 10 times the pressure humans apply when they shut their mouth.

*

An elephant's trunk contains 40,000 muscles. The human body has just 650 muscles.

*

The giant Marco Polo sheep have immensely long horns. The sheep, which live high in the mountains of Afghanistan, can have horns just over 6 feet, by far the longest of any sheep.

*

Bats and giraffes have the same number of vertebrae in their neck—seven. So do most other mammals. A swan has twenty-five.

*

The common wood frog is able to withstand the Arctic winter by turning itself into an ice cube. The frog allows two-thirds of its body water to freeze, thereby stopping its heart, brain, and breathing functions and slowing its metabolism to a crawl. As long as the frog's body temperature doesn't drop below about 20° Fahrenheit its body will survive on the glucose in its system until the spring thaw.

Similarly, some breeds of American alligators can survive the winter by freezing their snouts in ice, leaving their nostrils to breathe for months on end.

*

With food scarce in the lower regions of the oceans, animals have adapted accordingly. The umbrellamouth gulper eel has an extendable mouth and stomach so it can swallow prey that is bigger than itself.

*

Spiders can produce seven different types of silk. They range from the highly adhesive type used to trap prey to the incredibly strong threads spiders weave to support themselves. Most spiders can produce different types of silk, but no single spider is known to produce all seven.

*

Rhesus monkeys have handy little pouches in their cheeks. They use them to carry supplies of food they can snack on when hungry.

*

Sharks apparently are the only animals that never get sick. As far as is known, they are immune to every known disease including cancer. The shark also has the enviable ability to replace lost teeth in as little as twenty-four hours. It may use thousands of teeth over the course of a lifetime. The only handicap some sharks have is that they must swim constantly in order to "breathe" oxygen from water passing through their gills. They are also denser than water and will sink if they are stationery. Little wonder then that sharks do not sleep, they only take rests.

*

A rhinoceros beetle can support up to 850 times its own weight on its back. That would be the equivalent of a man carrying 76 family-sized cars on his back. If he is the strongman of the insect world, the spittle bug, or froghopper, is the ultimate athlete. A sap-sucking insect only about a quarter inch in length, the froghopper uses a catapult technique to spring itself more than 27 inches into the air. That's the equivalent of a human jumping to the height of a 689-foot tower. In doing this the insect generates a force that is 400 times that of gravity. (Humans leap with a force of around 2 or 3 times that of gravity and pass out when we experience anything over 5 gs of force.)

*

An ant can lift and carry in excess of 50 times its own weight.

*

Giant pandas have evolved a "sixth finger" to help them handle bamboo with greater dexterity. The thumblike

digit is an extension of the sesamoid bone in the wrist. It
can flex and work in conjunction with the real thumb to
help the panda grip the bamboo's stem and leaves.

*

Some animals are capable of generating their own light
through a process known as bioluminescence. The most
colorful example is a Brazilian worm that glows with a red
light on its head and green lights down its side. Its nickname is the railroad worm.

*

The Hawaiian bobtail squid has evolved a brilliantly clever
way of blending in with the seabed so as to avoid detection
by predators. The squid has a flashlight organ, made of sil-
ver reflector pads and luminescent bacteria, built into its
body. The squid uses the flashlight to hide its shadow, one
of the main clues predators use to find the heavily camou-
flaged creatures. Scientists are studying whether the flashlight organ can be replicated as a nanotechnology gadget.

*

Orchid bees are thought to be unique. They are the only
insects that suck up their food through a straw. Unlike the
rest of insects who lap up their food, the orchid bees
hoover up their nutrients via their long, funnel-like pro-
boscis.

*

A species of iguana on the Galapagos Islands can alter its
size according to the amount of food available. The
incredible shrinking marine iguana shortens itself by as
much as 20 percent when food is scarce. But when supplies are plentiful again it regrows to its original size. It is

the only known vertebrate to be able to deliberately yo-yo its weight like this.

*

Cobras aim right between their victims' eyes. Species like the Mozambique and black-necked spitting cobras can fire their venom with a force similar to that of a water pistol and can travel as far as 4 to 8 feet. Studies have shown they will generally only spit at a moving face.

*

Hyenas are equipped with one of the most powerful sets of teeth and jaws in the entire animal world. A ravenous pack of hyenas can turn a 992-pound zebra to little more than a few bones in under 25 minutes.

*

Giraffes wear the equivalent of surgical stockings. To get blood from their hearts to the rest of their elongated bodies, giraffes are equipped with a complex pumping system. Their heart is 2.5 times as big as that of any other animal of their size and siphons blood up to the brain with a force similar to that of a gas pump delivering fuel into a car. When a giraffe bends down to drink water or eat, however, a set of valves comes into operation ensuring the brain isn't suddenly flooded by blood, causing it damage. As part of this circulation system, giraffes also have very tight skin on their legs. Scientists think this is designed to ensure blood doesn't pool or clot as it makes the long journey down to the legs and back. The tight skin acts like a surgical stocking and squeezes the blood back up the body.

Creatures Great and Small:
Some of Nature's Davids
and Goliaths

The blue whale's blood vessels are so large a child could crawl through them.

*

The biggest spider is the goliath birdeater tarantula, from northeastern South America. The goliath can grow as big as a dinner plate and, as its name suggests, can steal birds from their nests.

*

The smallest spider is a mygalomorph from Borneo. It is no bigger than a pinhead.

*

The world's smallest known fish is a swamp-living creature from Sumatra called the paedocypris. Adults measure just ⅓ inch.

*

The world's smallest lizard comes from the Caribbean and is only ¾ inch long. It can curl up on a small coin like a dime or penny and is believed to be the smallest of all 23,000 known reptiles, birds, and mammals.

THE LARGEST KNOWN INSECTS, ACCORDING
TO THE SMITHSONIAN INSTITUTION:
  Ant: African driver ant, ⅓ inch long
  Beetle: South American longhorn beetle, 8 inches
      long
  Butterfly: white birdwing from the Solomon Islands,
      wingspan 12 inches
  Fly: South American robber fly, body length 2½
      inches
  Moth: Hercules emperor moth from New Guinea
      and Australia, wingspan 10½ inches

THE SMALLEST KNOWN INSECTS, ACCORDING TO
THE SMITHSONIAN INSTITUTION:
  Wasp: fairfly wasp, grows to a mere .0067 of an inch
      in length
  Ant: Sri Lankan ant, a mere ⅟₃₀ of an inch
  Beetle: feather-winged beetle, smaller than the
      period at the end of a sentence
  Butterfly: the South African dwarf blue, wingspan ½
      inch
  Moth: English micro-lepidopterna, wingspan ⅛ inch

*

Longevity is perhaps one of the clearest signs of successful
design, in which case the queen termite is one of nature's
real stars. These insects have the longest life span. They are
known to have lived for 50 years although some scientists
believe they are capable of living twice this long.

*

Sea urchins can live to around 200 years of age.

*

If you wanted to boil an ostrich's egg it would take you 40 minutes.

*

Few animals grow at a rate like the *Mola mola,* or giant ocean sunfish. The world's largest bony fish, the pebble-shaped *Mola* is only $\frac{1}{10}$ inch at birth. In the course of its life, however, it grows to a width of 14 feet and a length of 10 feet. Its adult weight is 4,000 pounds, which is 60 million times that at birth. That is a growth rate equivalent to a human baby growing to the size of six *Titanic*s.

Design Disasters:
Mother Nature's Greatest Misses

Many animals labor under severe physical handicaps. Pigs, for instance, have their eyes positioned on the sides of their heads, restricting their forward vision and making it physically impossible for them to look up into the sky. Similarly, owls have tubular-shaped eyeballs which can't be swiveled within their sockets. To see to the side they must move their entire heads. Fortunately, owls are able to rotate their heads 270 degrees. Cats are inhibited too. They can't see directly under their noses, which is why they can't find tidbits on the floor.

*

The shortest life span among vertebrates is thought to be that of a creature called *Nothobranchius furzeri,* a tiny, 2-inch-long fish from Africa. It goes through infancy, adolescence, adulthood, parenthood, and old age in the space of just six weeks.

*

The Basenji is the only breed of dog that doesn't bark.

The African dog, which dates back to the Egyptian pharaohs, has an unusually shaped larynx which prevents it from making the same noises as other dogs. It does, however, make a variety of sounds, including crowing, chortling, howling, growling, and yodeling. The Basenji usually make these sounds to signal it is happy.

*

The phrase "a red rag to a bull" is meaningless. Bulls, like many other animals, can only detect two pigments in the color spectrum, blue and a mix of red and green. The effect of this is that most things look a shade of gray. They charge at matadors because they are attracted to their dramatic, cape-waving gestures. The cape could be pink or bright yellow, it wouldn't make any difference.

*

Animals share many human ailments. Several breeds of dog, for instance, can get acne. Dogs with short coats, like boxers, bulldogs, and Doberman pinschers, are most susceptible. As with humans it normally appears on the face, specifically on the chin.

*

Dalmatians get a kind of gout. Uniquely among dogs they lack an enzyme called uricase which breaks down uric acid. As a result, the acid can build up in joints and cause kidney stones. Dogs who eat lots of red meat containing large amounts of a substance called purines are particularly at risk. As with humans, middle-aged males are most prone to the illness. Apes and guinea pigs are also susceptible to gout.

*

Some vets believe humans give cats asthma.

They can develop it from exposure to cigarette smoke, household dust, litter, and even human dandruff. Around 1 in 200 cats suffer from asthma, with Asian breeds like the Siamese and cats aged between one and five years most likely to develop it.

*

Domestic cats can suffer from passive smoking too. Studies have shown that cats who live with smokers double their risk of getting the feline equivalent of the cancer, non-Hodgkin's lymphoma.

*

Ferrets are particularly susceptible to human germs. They are one of the few species that catch colds from us.

*

Lemmings don't commit suicide—at least not in the way people think they do. The common idea that the rodents throw themselves off cliffs because of overcrowding is false. But the lemmings' habit of breeding in vast numbers does make them a magnet for hungry predators such as stoats, Arctic foxes, snowy owls, and a seabird, the long-tailed skua. As a result the lemming population in places like Greenland rises and falls spectacularly as they come under attack from land, sea, and air.

*

Big-bottomed sheep have a rare genetic condition. Researchers have discovered that sheep with unusually large hind ends have a gene that converts food into muscle rather than fat as it would normally do. The scientists named the gene callipyge. This is derived from a Greek word meaning "beautiful buttocks."

*

A lizard will become immobile and go into a trance if it is picked up and stroked between the eyes or turned over and rubbed on its belly. It is unclear whether this is a hypnotic state or whether the lizard is playing dead.

*

You can place a chicken in what seems to be a hypnotic state by tucking its head under its wing and moving it slowly in a circular motion.

*

A sheep can kill itself by rolling onto its back. This is a particular problem during the early summer, before shearing, when its heavy fleece becomes itchy. The sheep can't resist rolling onto its back to scratch itself, but such is the weight of the coat, it will not be able to roll back on to its feet. If left stranded like this it will die in one of two ways: magpies or gulls will come to pick out its eyes or it will develop "bloat," a deadly buildup of gases that swells up its stomach like a hot-air balloon.

*

Armadillos are the only animals other than humans who can suffer from leprosy.

*

Most insects are known to have some economic or environmental benefit to human society. It's estimated, for instance, that one-third of the world's crop production, worth $117 billion a year, relies on the pollination carried out by bees and other insects. The cockroach, however, is one of the very few insects with absolutely no benefit whatsoever.

*

Human pollutants have a bizarre effect on animals.
  Weedkiller turns male frogs into hermaphrodites but

also turns normally hermaphroditic fish into females. Starlings sing less when exposed to insecticides, while newts lose the ability to sniff out mates. DDT makes male gulls gay, while other chemicals have the ability to make goldfish hyperactive and monkeys fight rougher. Exposure to too much lead also makes gulls lose their balance and fall over.

*

Koalas have fingerprints that are almost identical to those of humans. Their fingers have the same complex combination of loops, whirls, and arches and are much more similar to ours than the prints of any chimpanzees. The eerie similarity is so great, they can cause confusion when Australian forensics experts scour crime scenes.

*

Two heads aren't better than one, at least if you are a snake.

Two-headed snakes are not uncommon. They grow the same way a human Siamese twin grows, when an embryo splits into identical twins but doesn't finish the process of separating.

The twins show very little brother or sisterly love. In fact, they fight constantly, mainly over food. When they catch prey they fight over who will swallow it, and if one catches the whiff of illicit food on the other head it will attack and try to swallow it whole. The two heads also fight over which direction to head in, which leaves them highly vulnerable to attacks by predators. Little wonder then that a twin-headed snake's chances of survival are generally zero.

*

The western gray kangaroo is known as the stinker kangaroo. Males give off a strange, curry-like smell. No one quite knows why.

Afterword

The more the natural world reveals itself, the more weird and wonderful it seems. The preceding pages have, hopefully, shed a little light on some of the more curious things we now know about the animal kingdom. But even stranger revelations lie in store. In the dark and uncharted depths of the ocean, for instance, it's thought that as much as 90 percent of life there remains waiting to be discovered by science. Elsewhere, the study of subjects such as animal intelligence, sensory perception, and communication is changing our view of non-human life at a precocious speed. Who knows what we will learn next? One thing is certain, however: life in all its infinite forms will continue to evolve in ways that—to the human mind, at least—seem sometimes awe-inspiring and other times utterly baffling. As the great geneticist J. B. S. Haldane famously wrote: "The universe is not only queerer than we suppose, but queerer than we can suppose."

Sources and References

ABBREVIATIONS

AB   *Animal Behavior*
ADW   Animal Diversity Web, University of Michigan
BL   *Biology Letters*
IW   *International Wildlife Magazine*, National Wildlife Federation (Aust.)
JEB   *Journal of Experimental Biology*
NG   *National Geographic*
NGN *National Geographic News*
Nften *Naturwissenschaften*
NS   *New Scientist*
PA   Press Association
PNAS *Proceedings of the National Academy of Sciences (U.S.)*
PRS *Proceedings of the Royal Society (U.K.)*
SA   *Scientific American*
SD   *Science Daily*
SI   Smithsonian Institution
SN   *Science News*
ZG   *ZooGoer*

PART ONE
TALK TO THE ANIMALS: THE CURIOUS ART OF ANIMAL COMMUNICATION

Body Talk:
How Animals Use Their Anatomies to Communicate

*Proceedings of the Royal Society (PRS)*B, vol. 271; Biology Letters 3, Feb 7, 2004, pp. 95–97; Aquatic Living Resources, 2003.
Discover, Aug. 2000.
Journal of Experimental Biology (JEB), vol. 203, 2000, pp. 765–71.
The Secret Life of Lobsters, T. Corson, HarperCollins, New York, 2004; *National Geographic (NG)*, Aug. 24, 2004.

Animal Behaviour (AB), vol. 57, p. 557.

Nature, vol. 373, no. 6513, Feb. 2, 1995, p. 425.

NG, July 8, 2002 and Mar. 23, 2005; *New Scientist (NS)*, issue 2112, Dec. 13, 1997; *Behavioral Ecology and Sociobiology*, vol. 59, no. 4, Feb. 2006.

Animal: The Definitive Visual Guide, ed. David Burnie, New York, Smithsonian Institution/London, Dorling Kindersley, 2001, p. 99; International Wildlife, Nat. Wildlife Federation, Sep./Oct. 1997.

NS, issue 2059, Dec. 7, 1996.

Network: Computation in Neural Systems, vol. 14, p. 321.

Vocal Heroes:
Birds, Whales, and Other Singing Stars

American Association for the Advancement of Science, Feb. 20, 2000, Washington, D.C., *Science* Jan. 5, 2001, vol. 291. no. 5501, pp. 52–54.

Science News (SN), vol. 157, no. 16, Apr. 15, 2000, p. 252.

Animal, Burnie, p. 341; *NG*, Dec. 9, 2003; *Houston Chronicle*, Feb. 21, 2003.

NS, issue 1812, Mar. 14, 1992.

NS, issue 1837, Sep. 5, 1992.

PRS B, vol. 269, no. 1493, Apr. 22, 2002, pp. 831–37.

SN, vol. 153, no. 13, Mar. 28, 1998.

Nature, vol. 411, no. 6835, May 17, 2001, p. 257.

National Geographic News (NGN), Mar. 3, 2006.

BMC Ecology, vol. 4, 2004.

PRS B, vol. 269, no. 1505, Oct. 22, 2002, pp. 2121–25.

AB online Feb. 15, 2006; *Science Now Daily News*, Feb. 23, 2006.

AB, vol. 57, p. 637.

Nature, vol. 409, no. 6817, Jan. 11, 2001, p. 139.

Science, vol. 308, no. 5730, Jun. 24, 2005, p. 1934; *NG*, June 23, 2005.

The Auk, vol. 120, Oct. 2003, p. 1062.

Science, vol. 291, no. 5501, Jan. 5, 2001, pp. 52–54; *Science Now*, Nov. 29, 2000.

Smithsonian National Zoological Park, www.nationalzoo.si.edu.

Whale Conservation Institute/Ocean Alliance, www.oceanalliance.org.

Journal of the Acoustical Society of America, June 2001; *NGN*, Mar. 30, 2005.

New Scientist, issue 1707, Mar. 10, 1990.

Nature, vol. 408, no. 6812, Nov. 30, 2000, p. 537.

Deep-Sea Research, vol. 51, p. 1889.

JEB, vol. 208, 2005, pp. 3121–31.

Science, vol. 289, no. 5483, Aug. 25, 2000, pp. 1310–11.

Public Library of Science Biology, Nov. 1, 2005.

Science Now, Nov. 21, 2001.

Naturwissenschaften (Nften) 89: pp. 352–356, Aug. 2002.

PRS B, vol. 264, no. 1386, Sep. 22, 1997, pp. 1355–61.

SN, vol. 153 no. 1, Jan. 3, 1998, p. 125; *JEB,* no. 208, 2005; Nature, vol. 420, no. 6915, Dec. 5, 2002, p. 475.

Nature, vol. 420, no. 6915, Dec. 5, 2002, p. 475.

Nature, vol. 411, no. 6834, May 10, 2001, p. 153.

Colorado State University, News Release, Jan. 26, 2001.

BBC Science & Nature homepage, www.bbc.co.uk/nature/wildfacts.

The Anthills Are Alive:
How Animals Buzz, Bang, Bounce, and Rap

Insect Fact and Folklore, Lucy W. Clausen, PhD, New York, The Macmillan Company, 1954, pp. 66–83; Sound Communication by Honeybees, Adrian M. Wenner, www.beesource.com; Zeitschrift für vergleichende Physiologic vol. 56, pp. 408–14.

SN, vol. 159, no. 12, Mar. 24, 2001, p. 190.

SN, vol. 157, no. 6, Feb. 5, 2000, p. 92.

NS, issue 1723, June 30, 1990.

NS, issue 1813, Mar. 21, 1992; *Behavioural Ecology and Sociobiology,* vol. 33, no. 3, Sept. 1993; *JEB,* vol. 208, 2005, pp. 3885–94.

JEB, vol. 208, 2005, pp. 647–59.

Science, vol. 274, no. 5284, Oct. 4, 1996, pp. 88–90.

NS, issue 1776, July 6, 1991.

Univ. of Florida, July 2004 in *Popular Science,* Jan. 2005, www.popsci.com.

Hot Gossip:
What Animals Talk About

Headless Males Make Great Lovers, Marty Crump, Chicago, Univ. of Chicago Press, 2005, pp. 152–54.

Current Biology, vol. 15, Oct. 11, 2005, pp. 1779–84.

Science, vol. 301, no. 5633, Aug. 1, 2003, p. 591.

SN, vol. 157, no. 6. Feb. 5, 2000, p. 92.

NS, issue 2451, June 12, 2004.

www.llamapaedia.com.

AB, vol. 28, p. 1070.

Smithsonian National Zoological Park, www.nationalzoo.si.edu.

Behavioral Ecology and Sociobology, vol. 51, no. 1, Dec. 2001, reported in SN, vol. 160, no. 20, Nov. 17, 2001, p. 312.

www.nationalgeographic.com.

Praxis Veterinaria, vol. 51, no. 3, 2003.

The Power of Speech:
Animals with Spectacular Voices

Proceedings: Biological Sciences, vol. 267, no. 1446, May 7, 2000.

Discover, Aug. 2000.

Proceedings of the National Academy of Sciences (PNAS), vol. 98, no. 20, Sep. 25, 2001, pp. 11371–75.

Smithsonian National Zoological Park, www.nationalzoo.si.edu/Animals/ AnimalRecords.

Info Sheet 177, Dept. of Systematic Biology, Entomology Section, National Museum of *Natural History*/Smithsonian Institution (SI: Ent 177).

Science, vol. 289, No. 5487, Sep. 22, 2000, pp. 2114–17.

Acoustical Society of America, Dec. 7 in *Science Daily (SD),* Dec. 29, 2000.

NGN, Nov. 7, 2005.

ZooGoer (ZG), Jan./Feb. 2000.

The Joy of Rex:
How Dogs and Other Animals Show They're Happy

NGN, Mar. 31, 2005.

Animal Behavior Society, Oregon, July 2001, in *SN,* vol. 160, no. 4, July 28, 2001, p. 55.

Animal: The Definitive Visual Guide to the World's Wildlife, Burnie, SI/London, Dorling Kindersley, p. 227.

The Smile of a Dolphin, Marc Bekoff, London, Discovery Books, 2000; *NS,* issue 2236, Apr. 29, 2000.

Dress Code:
What Animals Wear, and What It Tells Other Animals About Them

PRS B, vol. 269, no. 1499, July 22, 2002, pp. 1423–28.
NGN, Sep. 26, 2005.
SN, vol. 156, no. 24, Dec. 11, 1999, p. 375.
Nature, Vol. 409, no. 6818, Jan. 18, 2001, pp. 338–40.
AB, vol. 44, p. 63.
PRS B, vol. 269, no. 1488, Feb. 7, 2002, pp. 257–61.
PRS B, vol. 1265, no. 1405, Aug. 22, 1998, pp. 1515–20.
PRS B, vol. 273, no. 1589, Apr. 22, 2006, pp. 949–57.
Nature 410:204, Vol. 410, no. 6825, Mar. 8, 2001, p. 204.
The Oxford Companion to Animal Behaviour, ed. D. McFarland, Oxford, Oxford University Press, 1981, p. 14.
SN, vol. 153, no. 15, Apr. 11, 1998, p. 239.
Nature, vol. 415, no. 6875, Feb. 28, 2002, p. 975.

PART TWO
CREATURE COMFORTS: FOOD AND DRINK IN THE ANIMAL KINGDOM

You Are Who You Eat:
Who's Eating Who in the Animal World

Animal, Burnie, p. 280.
Journal of Chemical Ecology, vol. 20, p. 943.
Journal of Animal Ecology, vol. 59, p. 1091.
JEB, vol. 208, 2005, pp. 2227–36.
Animal, Burnie, p. 95.
AB, vol. 65, p. 385.
NGN, Oct. 11, 2005, and Feb. 9, 2006.
Jacobson's Organ and the Remarkable Nature of Smell, Lyall Watson, New York, W. W. Norton, 2000.
NS, issue 1744, Nov. 24, 1990.
Ockham's Razor, ABC, Radio National, Australia, Sep. 9, 2001.
Animal Diversity Web (ADW), Univ. of Michigan, animaldiversity. ummz.umich.edu.
Science World, Scholastic, Jan. 10, 1997.
Functional Ecology, vol. 4, p. 679.

Acquired Tastes:
Some Animal Likes and Dislikes

Animals, E. Hoffman, Mar. 1999.
Press Association (PA), Dec. 17, 2005.
NS, issue 2380, Feb. 1, 2003.
SN, vol. 147, no. 20, May 20, 1995, p. 316.
The Fats of Life, Caroline Pond, Cambridge University Press, 1998;
    reported in *NS,* Mar. 6, 1999.
PNAS, vol. 103, no. 11, Feb. 27, 2006, pp. 4152–56.
Mineralogical Society Bulletin, vol. 96, p. 3.
Oecologia, vol. 115, no. 3 pp. 331–36, July 1998.
Copeia, 1997, p. 593–95.
NGN, Feb. 18, 2005.
Public Library of Science Genetics DOI: 10.1371/journal.pgen.0010003.
www.vetinfo.com, Encyclopedia of Canine Veterinary Medical Informa-
    tion.
PRS B, vol. 270, no. 1522, July 7, 2003, pp. 1365–71.
Nature, vol. 427, no. 6971, Jan. 15, 2004, p. 212; *NS,* issue 2430, Jan. 17,
    2004.

Eating Disorders:
How Some Animals Starve and Others Binge

U.S. Dept. of Agriculture, Animal and Plant Inspection Service, Wildlife
    Services Report, Sep. 2002; Animal, Burnie, p. 280.
ZG, Jan./Feb., 2002.
JEB, vol. 208, 2005, pp. 113–27.
ADW.
SI: Ent 177, www.firstscience.com.
Headless Males, Crump, p. 96.
Whale Conservation Institute/Ocean Alliance, www.oceanalliance.org.
www.nationalgeographic.com.
NS, issue 2067, Feb. 1, 1997.
PA, Aug. 12, 2005.
Smithsonian National Zoological Park, 1999, www.nationalzoo.si.edu/ani-
    mals.
NS, issue 1758, Mar. 2, 1991.
ADW.

Calls of Nature:
Some Unpleasant Truths About Animal Bodily Functions

ZG, Nov./Dec. 2004.
Science, vol. 245, no. 4923, Sep. 15, 1989, p. 1236.
Polar Research, vol. 27, p. 56.
Ecology Letters, vol. 6, p. 361.
Comparative Animal Behaviour, Donald A. Dewsbury, London McGraw-
        Hill, 1978, p. 60.
U.N. Framework Convention on Climate Change, Information Sheet 22.
Report of the San Joaquin Valley United Air Pollution Control District,
        reported in *NGN,* Aug. 16, 2005; Research Nebraska, Mar. 2002.
NGN, May 13, 2002.
NGN, Mar. 14, 2006.
U.S. Dept. of Agriculture, Animal and Plant Inspection Service, Wildlife
        Services Report, Sep. 2002.
www.ratbehavior.org, 2003/2004.
Ibid.

Under the Influence:
Animals That Get Drunk and (Sometimes) Disorderly

Omni, Mar. 1986.
Ibid.
NS, issue 2426, Dec. 20, 2003.
Ibid.
Locoweed: Sandra Avant, College of Agriculture and Home Economics,
        New Mexico State University, 1998; *NS,* issue 2426, Dec. 20,
        2003.
Omni, Mar. 1986.
PA, Oct. 4, 2005.
PA, Feb. 6, 2006.
Nature Neuroscience, Feb. 2002.
PNAS, vol. 100, no. 8, Mar. 2003, pp. 4915–20.
Omni, Mar. 1986.
SN, vol. 156, no. 20, Nov. 13, 1999, p. 319.
Current Biology, vol. 8, p. 109.
SI: Ent 177.
Associated Press, Feb. 16, 2005.

Omni, Mar. 1986; *Physiological and Biochemical Zoology,* Mar./Apr. 2006.

Physiology & Behavior, vol. 63, no. 5, March 1998, pp. 739–44; *NS,* issue 1898, Nov. 6, 1993; *PNAS,* vol. 92, no. 19, Sep. 11, 1995, pp. 8990–93.

BBC Wildlife, vol. 24, no. 3, Mar. 2006.

Current Biology, vol. 16, p. 296.

PA, May 5, 2005.

PA, Jan. 16, 2006.

NS, issue 1736, Sep. 29, 1990.

Science, vol. 296, no. 5569, May 3, 2002, pp. 823–24.

NS, issue 2426, Dec. 20, 2003.

The Guardian, Nov. 11, 2005.

PART THREE
THE BIRDS AND THE BEES: ANIMALS AND THEIR LOVE LIVES

Looking for Mr. Right:
What Animals Want in Their Ideal Partner

1997 Margaret Morse Nice Lecture, reported in *The Wilson Bulletin,* 110(1), 1998.

PNAS, vol. 102, no. 21, May 9, 2005, pp. 7618–23.

PRS B, vol. 267, no. 1439, Jan. 22, 2000, pp. 165–69.

Natural History Magazine, Oct. 2004.

AB, vol. 40, p. 784.

Headless Males, Crump, p. 5.

Science, vol. 295, no. 5552, Jan. 4, 2002, p. 92.

PNAS, vol. 98, no.16, July 31, 2001, pp. 9171–76 *SN,* vol. 159, no. 9, Mar. 3, 2001, p. 135.

PRS B, vol. 272, no. 1572, Aug. 7, 2005, pp. 1541–46; Nature, vol. 423, no. 6935, May 1, 2003, pp. 31–32.

Behavioral Ecology and Sociobiology, vol. 53, no. 4, pp. 214–20, Mar. 2003.

PNAS, vol. 98, no. 23, Nov. 6, 2001, pp. 13155–60.

How Animals Have Sex, Gideon Defoe, London Weidenfeld & Nicolson, 2005.

Journal of Animal Behavior, vol. 53, p. 133.

Headless Males, Crump, p. 5; Animal Attraction: Cheaters, Channel Five, Feb. 1, 2006.

AB, vol. 40, p. 1185.

AB, vol. 39, p. 464.

AB, vol. 43, p. 865.

Ethology, vol. 111, pp. 810–20; PRS B, vol. 269, no. 1497, June 22, 2002, pp. 1233–39.

NGN, Aug. 4, 2005.

PNAS, vol. 99, no. 14, July 9, 2002, pp. 9290–93.

Nature, vol. 437, no. 7057, Sep. 15, 2005, pp. 408–11.

PRS B, vol. 270, no. 1522, July 7, 2002, pp. 1323–29.

The Art of Seduction:
How Animals Impress the Opposite Sex

Symposium of the California Academy of Sciences, San Francisco, Nov. 3, 2001, reported in *Science Now*, Nov. 7, 2001.

Principles of Animal Communication, Jack W. Bradbury and Sandra L. Vehren-camp, Cornell University, 1998.

Behavioral Ecology and Sociobiology, vol. 51, no. 6, May 2002; *NS*, issue 2389, Apr. 5, 2003.

SD online, Apr. 15, 2004.

AB, vol. 56, p 379.

NS, issue 2012, Jan. 13, 1996.

PRS, B, vol. 269, no. 1490, Mar. 7, 2002, pp. 475–48.

Comparative, Dewsbury, p. 84.

Science, vol. 292, no. 5526, June 29, 2001, pp. 2413–14.

Science, Jan. 21, 1994 vol. 263, no. 5145, p. 373.

Headless Males, Crump, p. 6.

AB, vol. 63, 2002, p. 907.

The Secret Life of Lobsters, T. Corson in NG, Aug. 24, 2004.

Headless Males, Crump, p. 160.

PNAS, vol. 98, no. 3, Jan. 30, 2001, pp. 1249–54.

Journal of Environmental Radioactivity, vol. 79, p. 1.

Brain Research, vol. 677, p. 82.

Ethology, vol. 105, p. 982.

AB, vol. 69, p. 529.

Animal Attraction: Cheaters, Channel Five, Television (UK), Feb. 1, 2006.

www.biopsychology.com, Feb. 14, 2006.

Ethology, vol. 103, p. 578.

Comparative, Dewsbury, p. 74.

Cetology, vol. 21, 1976, pp. 1–9.

International Ethological Conference, Honolulu, Aug. 1995 in *SN,* Oct. 21, 1995.

Headless Males, Crump, pp. 159–60.

NS, issue 2227, Feb. 26, 2000.

The Mating Game:
Sex in the Animal Kingdom

NGN, Feb. 13, 2004, extracted from *Dr. Tatiana's Sex Advice to All Creation: Definitive Guide to the Evolutionary Biology of Sex,* Olivia Judson, London Vintage, 2003, PA, Feb. 11, 2005.

Biological Exuberance: Animal Homosexuality and Natural Diversity, Bruce Bagemihl, New York, St. Martin's Press, 1999, www.firstscience.com.

American Bison, Dale F. Lott, Berkeley Univ. of California Press 2002, in NS, Aug. 31, 2002.

Seattle Times, Nov. 30, 2005.

How Animals Have Sex, Defoe.

PA, Sep. 14, 2005.

Nature, vol. 426, no. 6962, Nov. 6, 2003, p. 22.

NGN, Feb. 13, 2004.

ADW.

Info Sheet 146, SI, Dept. of Systematic Biology, Entomology Section.

NG online, Sep. 12, 2002.

Animal Attraction: Cheaters, Channel Five, Feb. 1, 2006.

Ibid.

Jacobson's Organ, Watson.

Smile of a Dolphin, Bekoff.

Animal Parts:
Some Curious Things About Sexual Organs

NG online, Feb. 13, 2004, extracted from Judson, *AB,* vol. 40, p. 374.

Nften, Nov. 15, 2001.

NG online, Sep. 12, 2002.

NGN, Oct. 23, 2001, citing *Nature,* Sep. 2001.

Animal Attraction: Cheaters, Channel Five, Feb. 1, 2006.

PNAS, vol. 101, no. 14, Apr. 6, 2004, pp. 4883–87.
How Animals, Defoe.
NS, issue 2176, Mar. 6, 1999.
PRS B, vol. 270, no. 1515, Mar. 22, 2003, pp. 649–52.
NS, issue 2072, Mar. 8, 1997.
NG online Feb. 13, 2004, extracted from *Dr. Tatiana,* Judson.

Dangerous Liaisons:
How Sex (or the Lack of It) Can Kill

Headless Males, Crump, pp. 18–19.
Science, vol. 271, no. 5245, Jan. 5, 1996, pp. 70–72.
SN, vol. 152, no. 12, Sep. 27, 1997.
SN, vol. 160, no. 6, Aug. 11, 2001, p. 93.
NS, issue 2051, Oct. 12, 1996.
American Zoologist, vol. 14, 1974.
JEB, vol. 208, 2005, pp. 595–601.
NS, issue 2525, Nov. 12, 2005.
NG online, Feb. 13, 2004, extracted from *Dr. Tatiana,* Judson.
Nature, vol. 423, no. 6943, June 26, 2003, p. 979.
PRS B, vol. 268, no. 1465, Feb. 22, 2001, pp. 407–11.
Animal Attraction: Cheaters, Channel Five, Feb. 1, 2006.
Biological Reviews of the Cambridge Philosophical Society, 71: pp.
      415–471. *The Auk,* Oct. 2000; Animal Attraction: Cheaters, Chan-
      nel Five, Feb. 1, 2006; AIDS, the Official Journal of the Interna-
      tional AIDS Society; Parasitology Today 8: pp. 159–66.
Nature, vol. 438, no. 7071, Dec. 22, 2005, p. 1097; *NS*, Feb. 11, 2006.
Animal Attraction: Cheaters, Channel Five, Feb. 1, 2006.
University of Minnesota, Academic Health Center, www.abc.umn.edu/rar/
      MNAALAS/ferret.html#Heat.

Good Breeding:
How Creatures Practice Birth Control

Nature, vol. 421, no. 6925, Feb. 20, 2003, p. 806.; *Science*, vol. 285, no. 5427,
      July 23, 1999, pp. 518–19.
Herpetological Natural History, vol. 5, p. 1.
PRS B, vol. 272, no. 580, Dec. 7, 2005, pp. 2475–78.

PRS B, vol. 271, Biology Letters 4, May 7, 2004, pp. 134–37.
PNAS, vol. 99, no. 2, Nov. 12, 2002, pp. 14897–902.
Biological Journal of the Linnean Society, vol. 50, p. 295; *NS*, issue 1919, Apr. 2, 1994.
NS, issue 1859, Feb. 6, 1993.
NS, issue 2029, May 11, 1996.
NS, issue 2091, July 19, 1997.
NS, issue 1785, Sep. 7, 1991; *SN*, Oct. 21, 1995.
NG online, Feb. 13, 2004, extracted from *Dr. Tatiana*, Judson.

As Queer as Folk:
Homosexuality in Animals

Biological Exuberance, Bagemihl.
Ibid.
SN, vol. 151, no. 1, Jan. 4, 1997.
NS, issue 2198, Aug. 7, 1999.
SN, vol. 153, no. 25, June 20, 1998.
NS, issue 1948, Oct. 22, 1994.
NG online, Feb. 13, 2004, extracted from *Dr. Tatiana*, Judson.
SN, vol. 15, no. 1, Jan. 4, 1997.
PA, Feb. 11, 2005.
Deinsea, vol. 8, 2001, pp. 243–47.

Till Death Do Us Part:
Fidelity and Infidelity in Animals

NG, Feb. 14, 2003; Feb. 13, 2004.
PNAS, vol. 99, no. 8, Apr. 16, 2002, pp. 5466–70.
Animal Attraction: Cheaters, Channel Five, Feb. 1, 2006.
U.S. Dept. of the Interior, news release, May 29, 2001.
AB, vol. 53, p. 1017.
NG online, Feb. 13, 2004.
NS, issue 2463, Sep. 4, 2004.
Current Biology, vol. 15, p. 1222.

PART FOUR
FAMILY AFFAIRS: THE TRIALS AND TRIBULATIONS OF ANIMAL PARENTHOOD

When the Stork Comes:
A Few Odd Facts About Animal Reproduction

Animal Conservation, vol. 5, p. 291.

International Wildlife Magazine (IW), Nat. Wildlife Federation, Sep./Oct. 1997.

Smithsonian National Zoological Park, 1999, www.nationalzoo.si.edu/animals.

www.firstscience.com.

Environmental Biology of Fishes, vol. 37, p. 213.

University of Washington, Seattle, www.staff.washington.edu/chudler/neurok.html; ADW.

Animal, Burnie, p. 447.

NGN, Jan. 26, 2004, and Feb. 2, 2003.

SN, vol. 157, no. 11, Mar. 11, 2000, p. 1681.

Science, vol. 292, no. 5516, Apr. 20, 2001, pp. 494–97.

Federation of American Societies for Experimental Biology, New Orleans, Apr. 21, 2002, reported in *Science Now,* Apr. 23, 2002.

Canadian Journal of Zoology, vol. 83, pp. 1343–45.

BBC Wildlife, vol. 24, no. 3, Mar. 2006.

www.nationalgeographic.com.

The Guardian, Notes & Queries, 2006; Joe Regenstein, MadSci Network, Zoology, www.madsci.org.

Animal, Burnie, p. 155.

SN, vol. 162, no. 5, Aug. 3, 2002, p. 78.

Chengdu Research Base of Giant Panda Breeding, China.

ZG, Mar./Apr. 1999.

NGN, Dec. 27, 2005.

Gestation Period table drawn from data at ADW.

Maternal Instincts:
Nature's Best (and Worst) Mothers

Whale Conservation Institute/Ocean Alliance, www.oceanalliance.org.

Nature, vol. 435, no. 7046, June 30, 2005, p. 1177.

NS, issue 2419, Nov. 1, 2003.

American Association for the Advancement of Science, Mar. 2006, reported on www.biopsychology.com.

Comparative, Dewsbury, p. 81.

NS, issue 2058, Nov. 30, 1996.

Journal of Animal Ecology, vol. 61, p. 681.

NS, issue 1915, Mar. 5, 1994.

Journal of Zoology, vol. 232, p. 691.

NS, issue 1792, Oct. 26, 1991 and issue 2351/2, Dec. 24/31, 2005.

AB, vol. 44, p. 753.

SN, vol. 159, no. 17, Apr. 28, 2001, p. 263.

Behavioral Ecology and Sociobiology, vol. 57, no. 3, Jan. 2005 in *NS,* issue 2467, Oct 2, 2004.

Tree Kangaroos of Australia and New Guinea, Roger Martin, at Univ. of Melbourne, CSIRO Publishing, 2005.

NS, issue 2222, Jan. 22, 2000.

Nature, vol. 416, no. 6882, Apr. 18, 2002, p. 733.

Science World, Scholastic, Jan. 10, 1997.

ADW.

AB, vol. 39, p. 496.

ZG, Mar./Apr., 1999.

Paternal Instincts:
Nature's Best (and Worst) Fathers

Biology Letters (BL), online, ref. 10 1098/rsbl. 2005. 0426.

NS, issue 2043, Aug. 17, 1996.

NG, June 18, 2004.

Ibid.

Ibid.

ZG, May/June, 1997.

NS, issue 1966, Feb. 1995.

NG online, Feb. 13, 2004, extracted from *Dr. Tatiana,* Judson.

Little Monsters:
Troublesome Children and How Animals Cope with Them

NS, issue 1920, Apr. 9, 1994.

Ibid.

NS, issue 2222, Jan. 22, 2000.

AB, vol. 41, p. 1097.

NS, issue 1920, Apr. 9, 1994.

PRS B, vol. 272, no. 1579, Nov. 22, 2005, pp. 2423–28.

PNAS, vol. 98, no. 15, July 17, 2001, pp. 8856–61.

SN, vol. 161, no. 16, Apr. 20, 2002, p. 250.

Behaviour, vol. 124, p. 57.

SN, vol. 153. no. 2, Jan. 10, 1998, p. 28.

A Death in the Family:
How Animals Cope with Loss

NS, issue 2066, Jan. 25, 1997.

Smile of a Dolphin, Bekoff.

Ibid.

NS, issue 2236, Apr. 29, 2000; *PRS* B, vol. 273, no. 1587, Mar. 22, 2006, pp. 707–712.

BL vol. 2, no. 1, Mar. 22, 2006, pp. 26–28; NS, issue 2236, Apr. 29, 2000.

Smile of a Dolphin, Bekoff.

Science, vol. 298, no. 5601, Dec. 13, 2002, pp. 2188–90.

PART FIVE
A MATTER OF LIFE AND DEATH: HOW THE FITTEST, STRONGEST, SMARTEST, AND DOWNRIGHT NASTIEST SURVIVE

No Holds Barred:
How Animals Fight

Wilkinson, F. A. 2001. An Aggressive Interaction Between Two Female Proechimys, Vida Silvestre Neotropical 21:x–x.

Animal, Burnie, p. 99; *IW,* Sep./Oct. 1997.

Society for Neuroscience, San Diego, Nov. 15, 2001, reported in *Science Now,* Nov. 19, 2001.

Science, vol. 155, no. 3765, Feb. 1967, pp. 1035–36.

NS, issue 1856, Jan. 16, 1993; AB, vol. 42, p. 171.

AB, vol. 70, p. 97.

Evolutionary Ecology, vol. 6, p. 254.

NS, issue 1957, Dec. 24, 1992.

Nature, Jan. 25, 2001, vol 409, no. 6819, p 475.
JEB, vol. 208, 2005, pp. 2865–72.
Oxford Companion of McFarland, p. 9.

Natural Born Killers:
Nature's Ultimate Hitmen

Science World, Scholastic, Jan. 10, 1997.
Environmental Biology of Fishes, 1998.
NS, issue 1997, Sep. 30, 1995.
Functional Ecology, vol. 8, p. 701.
NS, issue 1939, Aug. 20, 1994.
Science Now, Apr. 5, 2002.
The Birds of North America, no. 708, 2002.
www.nationalgeographic.com.
Nova, WGBH/PBS television, Apr. 28, 1998.
New England Journal of Medicine, vol. 340, pp. 1930, 1999.
Journal of Zoology, vol. 235, p. 587.
Headless Males, Crump, p. 93.
People and Nature Conservation Perspectives on Private Land Use and Endangered Species Recovery, Sydney, Surrey Beatty and Sons, 1995.

"I've Got You, I'm Under Your Skin":
How Parasites Kill Their Prey

Parasite Rex, Carl Zimmer, Touchstone, 2001.
PRS B, vol. 263, no. 1372, July 22, 1996, pp. 907–12.
Zimmer pp. 82–83.
PRS B, vol. 272, no. 1577, Oct. 22, 2005, pp. 2117–26.
PRS B, vol. 267, no. 1452, Aug. 7, 2000, pp. 1591–94.
NS, issue 2494, Apr. 9, 2005.
Nature, vol. 417, no. 6888, May 30, 2002, pp. 505–6.
NS, issue 2494, Apr. 9, 2005.
Nature, vol. 436, no. 7050, July 28, 2005, p. 476.

Liquids of Mass Destruction:
Deadly Weapons from the Animal Armory

Nature, vol. 434, no. 7036, Apr. 21, 2005, p. 973.

NS, issue 1724, July 7, 1990.

Headless Males, Crump, p. 125.

NS, issue 2420, Nov. 8, 2003.

Headless Males, Crump, p. 123.

PNAS, vol. 100, no. 3, Feb. 4, 2003, pp. 922–27.

Herpetoligica, 46, 1990, pp. 1–7.

NS, issue 1728, Aug. 4, 1990.

ADW.

NS, issue 2064, Jan. 11, 1997.

ZG, Jan./Feb., 2002.

Nature, vol. 423, no. 6940, June 5, 2003, p. 604.

NS, issue 2451, June 12, 2004.

Animal Attraction: Cheaters, Channel Five, Feb. 1, 2006.

Ibid.

Nature, vol. 398, no. 6723, Mar. 11, 1999, pp. 113–14.

Animal, Burnie, p. 245; Longleat Safari Park, Visitor Information.

NGN, Feb. 1, 2006.

Animal, Burnie, p. 492; *Tropical Topics,* no. 80, Jan. 2004.; ADW; NGN, Oct. 25, 2002.

David 1, Goliath 0:
A Few of Nature's Mismatches

Nften online, Nov. 1, 2002.

AB, vol. 57, p. 1301.

Snakes in Question, Carl Ernst and George Zug, Smithsonian Institution/CSIRO, 1996.

Ethology, vol. 94, p. 21.

Headless Males, Crump, p. 125.

Sunday Times, Review, Feb. 26, 2006, p. 12.

The Escape Artists:
Nature's Great Survivors

NS, issue 1702, Feb. 3, 1990.
Headless Males, Crump, pp. 116–17.
Ibid., Dec. 4, 1997, p. 116.
Nature, vol. 390, no. 6659, p. 453.
Science, vol. 302, no. 5647, Nov. 7, 2003, p. 1007.
Smithsonian National Zoological Park, Animal Index, www.nationalzoo.si.edu.
ADW.
Ibid.
Terra, vol. 31: pp. 30–34, 1993.
Nature, vol. 433, no. 7026, Feb. 10, 2005, p. 624.
Animal, Burnie, p. 27.
Science, vol. 134, no. 3493, Dec. 8, 1961, pp. 1873–76; vol. 139, no. 3550, Jan. 11, 1963, pp. 116–18.
The Science Channel, www.science.discovery.com; CBS News, The Odd Truth, Apr. 15, 2005, www.cbsnews.com.

And the Oscar Goes to . . . :
How Animals Act Their Way Out of Trouble

NS, issues 2445 and 2448, May 1 and 22, 2004.
SI: Ent 177.
NGN, Feb. 10, 2005.
Behavioral Ecology vol. 11, no. 2, March 2000: pp. 169–77.
NS, issue 1861, Feb. 20, 1993.
Science, vol. 243, No. 4891, Feb. 3, 1989, p. 643.
Science, vol. 307, no. 5717, Mar. 25, 2005, p. 1927.
PRS B, vol. 268, no. 1478, Sep. 7, 2001, pp. 1755–58.
PRS B, vol. 272, no. 1569, June 22, 2005, pp. 1203–07.

SOURCES AND REFERENCES 285

PART SIX
WORK, REST, AND PLAY: ANIMAL LIFESTYLES

Six (or Eight) Feet Under:
Some Animal Occupations

PRS B, vol. 269, no. 1505, Oct. 22, 2002, pp. 2087–93.
SN, vol. 152, no. 12, Sep. 27, 1997, p. 200.
NS, issue 20466, Sep. 7, 1996.
Comparative, Dewsbury, p. 59.
American Journal of Botany vol. 88, Oct. 2001, pp. 1768–73.
IW, Sep./Oct. 1997.
Philosophical Transactions of the Royal Society of London, Series B, vol. 342, p. 161.
ZG, 28(2) 1999.
Journal of Animal Ecology, vol. 61, p. 225.
SI: Ent 177.

Workers of the Ant World Unite:
Nature's Jack-of-All-Trades

NS, issue 1709, Mar. 24, 1990.
BBC World Service, *Discovery*, reported BBC News, Mar. 18, 2004; *Scientific American* (SA), Jan. 6, 2006 and Sep. 22, 2005; *Nature*, vol. 437, no. 7058, p. 495; *NGN*, Sep. 2001, 2005.
Crump, p. 103.
Crump, p. 102.
Nature, vol. 430, no. 7073, Jan. 12, 2006, p. 153.
BBC World Service, *Discovery*, reported BBC News, Mar. 18, 2004.

Skilled Labor:
Animals That Use Tools

Folia Primatologica, vol. 54, p. 100.
Public Library of Science Biology, DOI: 10.1371/journal.pbio.0030380.
SN, vol. 157, no. 6, Feb. 5, 2000, p. 92; *NS*, issue 1960, Jan. 14, 1995.
Nature, vol. 411, no. 6838, June 7, 2001, p. 654.

Science, vol. 297, no. 5583, Aug. 9, 2002, p. 981; *PRS* B 270: pp. 867–74, Apr. 22, 2002.

SN, vol. 158, no. 18, Oct. 28, 2000, p. 284.

Crump, p. 86.

No Place Like Home:
How Animals Find Their Domestic Bliss

NS, issue 2222, Jan. 22, 2000.

Journal of Natural History, vol. 28, p. 731.

NS, issue 2222, Jan. 22, 2000.

SI: Ent 177.

Nature, vol. 426, no. 6964, Nov. 20, 2003, p. 243.

NGN, June 20, 2002.

PRS B, vol. 269, no. 1505, Oct. 22, 2002, pp. 2087–93.

American Society for Microbiology, May 2004 in *NS*, issue 2450, June 5, 2004.

Behavioral Ecology, vol. 13, no. 3, pp. 381–85, May 2002.

Nature, vol. 392, no. 6676, Apr. 9, 1998, p. 558.

NS, issue 2483, Jan. 22, 2005; American Ornithologists' Union, Aug. 2001.

Nature, vol. 431, no. 7004, Sep. 3, 2004, p. 39.

Biologist, Dec. 2002.

ZG 31(2) 2002; Geophysical Research Letters, vol. 21, p. 995.

PRS, vol. 265, no. 1404, Aug. 7, 1998, pp. 1407–10.

Beauty and the Beasts:
Health, Hygiene, and Beauty in the Animal World

PRS B, vol. 269, no. 1505, Oct. 22, 2002, pp. 2135–39.

Nature, vol. 416, no. 6883, Apr. 25, 2002, p. 807.

NS, issue 2222, Jan. 22, 2000.

Ibid.

Journal of Chemical Ecology, vol. 26, p. 2781; *Nften*, vol. 90, p. 301.

Psychoneuroendocrinology, vol. 14, p. 155.

www.nationalgeographic.com.

Science, vol. 297, no. 5585, Aug. 23, 2002, pp. 1255–56.

Canadian Journal of Zoology, vol. 80, Mar. 2002, pp. 471–78.

Behavioral Ecology, vol. 12, no. 4, July 2001, pp. 429–38.

Journal of Experimental Marine Biology and Ecology, vol. 203, p. 245.

South African Journal of Geology, vol. 95, p. 74.

Science, vol. 307, no. 5706, Jan. 7, 2005, pp. 111–13; *NGN*, Jan. 6, 2005.

JEB, vol. 208, 2005, pp. 233–48.

Nature, vol. 429, no. 6990, May 27, 2004, p. 363.

Rip Van Winkles:
How Animals Get Their Heads Down

SN, vol. 152, no. 19, Nov. 8, 1997; *Neuroscience & Biobehavioral Reviews*, vol. 9, issue 2, summer 1985.

SA online edition, Feb. 2, 1998.

SA online edition, Feb. 2, 1998; *Nature*, 397, Feb. 4, 1999.

Nature, vol. 397, no. 6718, Feb. 4, 1999, pp. 397–98.

Ibid.; www.birdweb.org.

www.nationalgeographic.com.

The Science Channel, www.science.discovery.com.

New York Times, July 4, 1995.

Discover, Aug. 2000.

SN, vol. 161, no. 16, Apr. 20, 2002, p. 250.

PRS B, vol. 271, Biology Letters 6, Dec. 7, 2004, pp. 468–70.

Ecological Society of America and the Society for Ecological Restoration, Tucson, Aug. 6, 2002, reported in *Science Now*, Aug. 7; *Science*, vol. 287, no. 5459, Mar. 10, 2000, pp. 1834–37.

Nature, vol. 437, no. 7063, Oct. 27, 2005, pp. 1253–86.

NS, issue 2426, Dec. 20, 2003.

Nature, vol. 409, no. 6823, Feb. 22, 2001, p. 997.

JEB, vol. 200, 1997 pp. 467–75.

PNAS, vol. 85, no. 21. Nov. 1, 1988, pp. 8350–54.

Science, vol. 244, no. 4912, June 30, 1989, p. 1593.

Nature, vol. 429, no. 6994, June 24, 2004, p. 825.

Moose Surf, Dragons Play Frisbee:
How Animals Get Stressed, and How They Unwind

Society for Neuroscience, Nov. 15, 2005 in the *Guardian*, Nov. 16, 2005.

Biological Conservation, vol. 128, p. 501.

Association for the Study of Animal Behaviour, in *NS*, issue 2128, Apr. 4, 1998.

Human Nature, vol. 13, no. 3, 2002, pp. 383–89.

International Journal of Primatology, vol. 18, p. 455.

International Council for the Exploration of the Seas, October, 1994, in *NS,* issue 1959, Jan. 7, 1995.

www.nationalgeographic.com.

Smile of a Dolphin, Bekoff.

Journal of the Lepidopterists' Society, vol. 56, no. 2, 2002, pp. 90–97.

SN, vol. 159, no. 13, Mar. 31, 2001, p. 199.

PRS B, vol. 271, no. 1552, Oct. 7, 2004, pp. 2077–84.

Science Now, July 5, 2001.

NS, issue 2424, Dec. 6, 2003.

SN, vol. 162, no. 5, Aug. 3, 2002, p. 78.

PA, Feb. 1, 2006.

The Natural History of Mammals, F. Bourliere, New York, Knopf, 1964.

PART SEVEN
SOCIAL ANIMAL: HOW CREATURES LIVE TOGETHER

All for One, and One for All:
How Animals Look Out for Each Other

Headless Males, Crump, pp. 150–54.

NS, issue 2538, Feb. 11, 2006.

PRS B, vol. 271, Biology Letters 5, Aug. 7, 2004, pp. 281–82.

SN, vol. 160, no. 11, Sep. 15, 2001, p. 172.

NS, issue 2176, Mar. 6, 1999.

Sperm Whales: Social Evolution in the Ocean, Hal Whitehead, Chicago, Univ. of Chicago Press, 2004.

Biological Journal of the Linnean Society, vol. 52, p. 163.

PNAS, vol. 99, no. 9, Apr. 30, 2002, pp. 6075–79.

AB, vol. 54, p. 89

Science, vol. 302, no. 5645, Oct. 24, 2003, pp. 634–36; *NGN,* Oct. 23, 2003; *Science,* vol. 293, no. 5539, Sep. 28, 2001, pp. 2446–49.

Molecular Ecology, vol. 12, p. 743, Mar. 2003.

AB, vol. 44, p. 111.

Headless Males, Crump, pp. 150–54.

Wildfowl & Wetlands Trust, www.wwt.org; *Planet Earth,* BBC TV, Mar. 5, 2006.

PA, Feb. 2, 2006 and Mar. 10, 2005.

PA, Apr. 21, 2005, and May 5, 2005.
CBS News/Associated Press, Feb. 23, 2006.

Government, for the Animals, by the Animals:
Politics, Power, and Police States

SN, vol. 167, no. 12, Mar. 19, 2005, p. 184; *Nature*, 4 vol. 419, no. 6902,
     Sep. 5, 2002, pp. 61–65.
NS, issue 2291, May 19, 2001.
Nature, vol. 439, no. 7075, Jan. 26, 2006, p. 426.
PRS B vol. 268, no. 1472, June 7, 2001, pp. 1139–46.
Ibid.
NS, issue 2494, Apr. 9, 2005.
PRS, B. vol. 271, BL Supplement 6, Dec. 7, 2004, pp. 477–81.
PRS B vol. 269, no. 1492, Apr. 7, 2002, pp. 721–27.
Journal of Neuroscience, vol. 17, p. 6463.
Public Library of Science Biology, DOI: 10.1371/journal.pbio.0030363.

Codfathers:
How Animals Behave Like the Mafia

NS, issue 2197, July 31, 1999.
The Secret Life of Lobsters, T. Corson in NG, Aug. 24, 2004.
NS, issue 2519, Oct. 1, 2005.
Ecological Society of America, Aug. 7, 2001 in *Science Now,* Aug. 8, 2001.
Society for Experimental Biology, Apr. 2004 in *NS*, issue 2441, Apr. 3, 2004.
Behavioral Ecology and Sociobiology, vol. 30, no. 3/4, April 1992, p. 201; *Ethology,* vol. 91, p. 147.
Nineteenth Meeting of the American Ornithologists' Union, Seattle,
     Aug. 15–18, 2001.
NS, issue 2519, Oct. 1, 2005.

It's a Woman's World:
How the "Weaker" Sex Run the Ultimate Matriarchal Societies

Science Now, Oct. 16, 2002; NG online, Feb. 13, 2004.
Nature, vol. 389, no. 6650, Oct. 2, 1997, p. 450.

NG online, Feb. 13, 2004; *PRS* B, vol. 270, no. 1521, June 22, 2003,
    pp. 1247–54, *Behavioral Ecology*, Mar. 2002.
Science, vol. 292, no. 5526, June 29, 2001, pp. 2479–82.

PART EIGHT
NOT-SO-DUMB ANIMALS: WHY CREATURES ARE MORE INTELLIGENT THAN YOU THINK

Two Bees or Not Two Bees?
Animals That Can Put Two and Two Together

NS, issue 2431, Jan. 24, 2004.
Science, vol. 282, no. 5389, Oct. 23, 1998, pp. 746–49.
AB, vol. 49, p. 159.
The Journal of Comparative Psychology, July 2005, reported in *SD*, July 11,
    2005.
PNAS, vol. 102, no. 46, Nov. 15, 2005, pp. 16870–74.
SD online, July 11, 2005.
Nature, vol. 421, no. 6919, Jan. 9, 2003, p. 160.
JEB, vol. 208, 2005, pp. 2903–12.
Nature, vol. 420, no. 6912, Nov. 14, 2002, p. 171.
Journal of Experimental Psychology: Applied Behaviour Processes, vol. 31,
    p. 95.
Nature, vol. 425, no. 6955, Sep. 18, 2003, p. 297.

I Remember Ewe:
Why Elephants Aren't the Only Animals Who Don't Forget

NS, issue 2451, June 12, 2004.
NGN, July 19, 2005.
Animal Cognition, vol. 4, p. 109.
SN, Apr. 25, 1992.
www.thenakedscientists.com.
Science, vol. 304, no. 5677, June 11, 2004, pp. 1682–83.
Dog ranking: *The Intelligence of Dogs: Canine Consciousness and Capabilities*,
    Stanley Coren, London, Bantam, 1995.
NGN, Oct. 27, 2005.
Journal of Experimental Psychology: General, Sept. 2000.

Nature, vol. 395, no. 6699, Sep. 17, 1998, p. 272.

Science, vol. 292, no. 5516, Apr. 20, 2001, pp. 417–19.

Nature, vol. 406, no. 6794, July 27, 2000, p. 404.

NS, issue 2529, Dec. 10, 2005.

Behavioral Neuroscience, Oct. 2003.

Knock, Knock, Who's Bear?
The Cunning (and Criminal) Workings of the Animal Mind

PA, July 6, 2005.

IW, Sep./Oct. 1997.

Nature, vol. 405, no. 6782, May 4, 2000, pp. 35–36.

Nften, 87, 563, Dec. 2000.

Daily Telegraph, online news, Jan. 5, 2006.

NGN, Dec. 9, 2004.

NGN, Dec. 9, 2004; *ZG,* Nov./Dec. 2005.

The Journal of the Acoustical Society of America, vol. 119, p. 620.

NS, issue 2483, Jan. 22, 2005.

U.S. Animal Behavior Society, Aug. 2005.

NGN, May 2, 2005.

PRS B, vol. 268, no. 1467, Mar. 22, 2001, pp. 565–71.

Nature, vol. 422, no. 6931, Apr. 3, 2003, p. 495.

McFarland, p. 16.

Current Biology, vol. 15, Jan. 11, 2005, pp. 64–67, reported in *NGN,* Feb. 14,
    2005.

NS, issue 2511, Aug. 8, 2005.

Copeia, 1986, pp. 1001–4.

NS, issue 1681, Sep. 9, 1989.

NS, issue 1715, May 5, 1990.

NS, issue 1774, June 22, 1991.

Nften, vol. 91, p. 245.

Nature, vol. 414, no. 6862, Nov. 22, 2001, pp. 443–46.

Nature, vol. 417, no. 6888, May 30, 2002, pp. 505–06.

Animal Cognition, vol. 7, p. 69.

PRS B, vol. 271, no. 1549, Aug. 22, 2004, pp. 1693–99.

PART NINE
BASIC INSTINCTS: EXTRAORDINARY ANIMAL POWERS

Hear All Evil:
How Animals See, Smell, Hear, and Echolocate

University of Washington, Seattle, www.staff.washington.edu/chudler/
    neurok.html.
Ibid.; *SA*, Apr. 2001, p. 24.
Praxis Veterinaria, vol. 51, no. 3, 2003.
NGN, June 23, 2004.
NS, issue 2499, May 14, 2005.
Longleat Safari Park.
Science, vol. 293, no. 5536, Sep. 7, 2001, pp. 1845–48.
Info Sheet 177, Dept. of Systematic Biology, Entomology Section,
    National Museum of Natural History/Smithsonian Institution.
The Science Channel, www.science.discovery.com.
JEB, vol. 208, 2005, pp. 3645–54.
SN, vol. 157, no. 6, Feb. 5, 2000, p. 92.
Journal of Herpetology, vol. 30, p. 347.
Comparative Hearing: Mammals, Fay and Popper, Springer-Verlag, 1994;
    ADW.
Praxis Veterinaria, vol. 51, no.3, 2003.
Comparative Hearing: Mammals, Fay and Popper.
Nature, vol. 411, no. 6840, June 21, 2001, p. 908, Longleat Safari Park.
PRS B, Vol. 271, *Biology Letters* 6, Dec. 17, 2004, pp. 485–87; *NS*, Nov. 2,
    2002, issue 2367.
University of Washington, Seattle, www.staff.washington.edu/chudler/
    neurok.htm.
Ibid.
PNAS, vol. 98, no. 13, June 19, 2001, pp. 7371–74.
Current Biology, vol. 10, Jan. 15, 2000, p. 115–17.
Behavioral Ecology and Sociobiology, vol. 28, no. 6, Nov. 2004.
The Science Channel, www.science.discovery.com.
Jacobson's Organ, Watson.
Ibid.
Science, vol. 311, no. 5761, Feb. 3, 2006, pp. 666–70.
Nften, vol. 87, p. 83.
Applied AB Science, reported in *Sunday Times*, News Review, Nov. 6,
    2005.

Chemical Senses, vol. 28, p. 279.
Nature, vol. 417, no. 6886, May 16, 2002, p. 241.
JEB, vol. 208, 2005, pp. 461–68.
ADW.
Science, vol. 310, no. 5752, Nov. 25, 2005, pp. 1260–61.
NS, issue 2485, Feb. 5, 2005.

Southpaws:
How Some Animals Lead with Their Left

Applied AB Science, DOI:10.1016/j.applanim.2004.11.00.
BMC Ecology 2003 3:8, Oct. 23, 2003.
AB, vol. 117, p. 281; *NS,* issue 1989, Aug. 5, 1995; *Nature,* vol. 414, p. 707,
    Dec. 13, 2001; Whale Conservation Institute/Ocean Alliance,
    www.oceanalliance.org.
Science, vol. 278, no. 5337, Oct. 17, 1997, pp. 483–86.
AB, vol. 39, p. 1224.
AB, vol. 56, p. 875.
Journal of Mammalogy, vol. 72, p. 823.

Animal Doctors:
How Creatures Can Heal Themselves (and Others)

SN, vol. 138, Nov. 3, 1990.
ZG, Jan./Feb. 1998.
Ibid.
NS, issue 2222, Jan. 22, 2000; *SN,* vol. 138, Nov. 3, 1990.
NS, issue 1691, Nov. 18, 1989.
AB, vol. 39, p. 797, *NS,* issue 1809, Feb. 22, 1992.
Emu (Australia), vol. 97, p. 248.
Sunday Times, News Review, Nov. 6, 2005.
Neurology, vol. 62, 2004, pp. 2303–05.
Current Directions in Psychological Science, vol. 12, pp. 236, Dec. 2003.
ADW.
NGN, Oct. 24, 2003.
NGN, June 1, 2004 and June 14, 2005.
NS, issue 1823, May 30, 1992.

Unearthly Powers:
How Animals Use Their Sixth Sense

Science, vol. 208, no. 4445, May 16, 1980, pp. 695–96.
Eos, no. 58, 1977, p. 254.
NG online, Jan. 4, 2005.
Florida Museum of Natural History, release, Dec. 30, 2004.
Praxis Veterinaria, vol. 51, no. 3, 2003.
NS, issue 2092, July 26, 1997.

PART TEN
DO THE LOCOMOTION: HOW ANIMALS GET FROM A TO B

Poetry in Motion:
Nature's Greatest Movers

IW, Sep./Oct. 1997.
Alaska Science Forum, Mar. 24, 1981; *JEB,* vol. 209, 2006, pp. 590–98.
NS, issue 2436, Feb. 28, 2004.
Smithsonian National Zoological Park, Animal Index, www.nationalzoo.
    si.edu.
NG Channel, Mar. 29, 2004.
Oxford Companion, McFarland, p. 349.
NS, issue 2023, Mar. 30, 1996.
The Trail of the Snail, Arno Brosi, www.members.tripod.com/arnobrosi/
    snail.html.
PNAS, vol. 100, no. 19, Sep. 16, 2003, pp. 10603–6.
Animal, Burnie, p. 97.
Nature, vol. 418, no. 6898, Aug. 8, 2002, pp. 603–4.
The Science Channel, www.science.discovery.com.
SN, vol. 162, no. 17, Oct. 26, 2002.
Environmental Biology of Fishes, vol. 36, p. 157.
NGN, Apr. 27, 2004.
SI: Ent 177.
www.nationalzoo.si.edu/Animals/AnimalRecords.
Smithsonian National Zoological Park, Animal Index, www.nationalzoo.
    si.edu.

Globe-Trotters:
Long-Distance Animals

NS, issue 1980, June 3, 1995.
Nature, vol. 343, no. 6260, Feb. 22, 1990, p. 746.
The Auk, vol. 115, no. 1, Jan. 1998, p. 196–203.
NS, issue 1720, June 9, 1990.
Reuters, Jan. 25, 2006.
Nature, vol. 395, no. 6702, Oct. 8, 1998, p. 556.
Nature, vol. 421, no. 6923, Feb 6, 2003, p. 599.
PNAS, vol. 96, no. 24, Nov. 23, 1999, pp. 13845–46; *NGN*, Jan. 29, 2004.
NGN, Jan. 29, 2004; *Science*, vol. 248, May 11, 1990, p. 724–27.
Jacobson's Organ, Watson.
Nature, vol. 421, no. 6918, Jan. 2, 2003, pp. 60–63.
SI: Ent 177.
PNAS, vol. 100, no. 10, May 13, 2003, pp. 5863–66.

Are We There Yet?:
Some Poor Animal Travelers

Animal, Burnie, p. 242.
NS, issue 2402, July 5, 2003.
Joey Green's Gardening Magic, Emmaus, Pennsylvania, (U.S.) Rodale Books, 2003.
SN, vol. 161, no. 16, Apr. 20, 2002, p. 250.
Behavioral Ecology and Sociobiology, vol. 43, no. 3, August 1998, in *NS*, issue 2133, May 9, 1998.

PART ELEVEN
CHILDREN OF THE EVOLUTION: NATURE'S SUCCESSES AND FAILURES

Design Classics:
Mother Nature's Greatest Hits

JEB, vol. 205, 2002, pp. 1189–97.
Longleat Safari Park.
NG Channel, Mar. 29, 2004.
Nature, vol. 340, no. 6231, July 27, 1989, p. 305.

Nature, vol. 373, no. 6511, Jan. 19, 1995, pp. 244–46.

Science, vol. 285, no. 5427, July 23, 1999, pp. 518–19.

NS, issue 2069, Feb. 15, 1997.

Field & Stream, vol. 98, issue 3, July 1993, p. 21.

Nature, vol. 414, no. 6859, Nov. 1, 2001, p. 33.

The Science Channel, www.science.discovery.com.

Ibid.

NGN, Mar. 7, 2006.

Nature, vol. 242, no. 5399, Apr. 20, 1973, p. 509.

Science, vol. 285, no. 5427, July 23, 1999, pp. 518–19.

Nature, vol. 389, no. 6649, Sep. 25, 1997, p. 343; *NGN,* Mar. 1, 2005;
    American Alligator, Univ. of Georgia, Savannah River Ecology
    Laboratory, www.uga.edu.

Checklist of the fishes of the eastern tropical Atlantic, JNICT, Lisbon; SEI,
    Paris; and UNESCO, Paris, vol. 1, 1990, p. 206.

NGN, June 23, 2004.

SN Online, Mar. 15, 1997.

NGN, June 13, 2005; *Oxford Guide,* McFarland, p. 349.

Smithsonian National Zoological Park, www.nationalzoo.si.edu.

SI: Ent 177.

Animal, Burnie, p. 191.

EENY, University of Florida, 332, Dec. 2004, www.creatures.ifas.ufl.edu.

Science, vol. 303, no. 5655, Jan. 9, 2004, pp. 235–38.

Science Now, Dec. 12, 2003.

Nature, vol. 403, no. 6765, Jan. 6, 2000, p. 37.

NGN, Feb. 10, 2005.

SN, vol. 161, no. 17, Apr. 27, 2002, p. 267.

NS, issue 2100, Sep. 20, 1997; *Animal,* Burnie, p. 243.

Creatures Great and Small:
Some of Nature's Davids and Goliaths

Whale Conservation Institute/Ocean Alliance, www.oceanalliance.org.

NGN, June 23, 2004.

Ibid.

BBC News, Jan. 25, 2006; *PRS* B, vol. 273, no. 1589, Jan. 2006, pp.
    895–99.

Caribbean Journal of Science, Dec. 2001.

Largest and Smallest: SI: Ent 177.

Ibid.
U.S. Fishery Bulletin, Oct. 2003.
Longleat Safari Park.
NGN, Feb. 2, 2003.

Design Disasters:
Mother Nature's Greatest Misses

ADW; Animal, Burnie, p. 316.
NS, issue 2404, July 19, 2003.
Basenji Club of America, www.basenji.com.
University of Washington, Seattle, www.staff.washington.edu/chudler/
    eyecol.html.
Encyclopedia of Canine Veterinary Medical Information, www.vetinfo.
    com.
The Pet Health Library, www.VeterinaryPartner.com.
NGN, Oct. 25, 2005.
American Journal of Epidemiology, no. 156, Aug. 1, 2002, pp. 268–73.
www.suevet.com.
Science, vol. 302, no. 5646, Oct 31, 2003, pp. 866–68.
Genome Research, Oct. 2002.
Crump, p. 114.
A. Brown, firsthand experience, Wales, c. 1975.
A Shepherd's Watch, D. Kennard, London, Headline Publishers, 2004.
Science, vol. 308, no. 5724, May 13, 2005 pp. 1040–42.
ADW, SI Dept of Systematic Entomology, www.entomology.si.edu.
AB, vol. 68, p. 465; *SN*, vol. 161, no. 16, Apr. 20, 2002, p. 243; *SN*, vol.
    162, no. 19, Nov. 9, 2002.
NS, issue 2059, Dec. 7, 1996.
NGN, Mar. 22, 2002.
IW, Sep. Oct. 1997.

Author's Note
and Acknowledgments

My first thanks must go to my agent Mary Pachnos at Gillon Aitken Associates. It was Mary's idea that I should write "a little book of strange animal facts" and from the very outset she, along with everyone else at the agency—in particular Gillon Aitken and Sally Riley but also Dea Brovig and James Pusey—has been a source of huge encouragement. I am grateful to them all.

Starting work on the book I set myself some ground rules. Facts should be rooted in sound scientific sources but not so complex as to be daunting to the nonscientific reader. There should be no urban myths, and, as much as possible, behavior should be drawn from the natural rather than the human world. If, here and there, I have strayed from one or two of these principles it has only been to deliver a tidbit that was simply too good to miss. (For instance, the facts that bears can trick people into opening their front doors and that circus elephants are partial to vodka were both reported by reputable news agencies rather than learned journals. Apologies to those of you of a pedantic disposition.)

In trying to achieve this aim, my most helpful ally was Dr. Steven Le Comber, an evolutionary biologist at the School of Biological and Chemical Sciences, Queen

Mary, University of London. Whether it was furnishing me with the latest copy of the *Journal of Experimental Biology* or directing me to the world expert on insect methane emissions—who, sadly, dismantled an urban myth that cockroaches break wind every fifteen minutes—Steve was an ever ready and enthusiastic source of scientific sense. He, incidentally, is part of the team that discovered grandmother bats share the same sexual male partner as their granddaughters. He explained the extremely convoluted family relationships produced by this intergenerational breeding. Fascinating though these details were, they clearly fell into the "too complex" category. My brain hurt for days afterwards.

My other major vote of professional thanks must go to my editor and publisher, Francesca Liversidge at Transworld. Her guidance, good sense—and frequently fruity humor—were priceless as I shaped up the disparate collection of facts I had amassed. At my American publishers, the Free Press in New York, Martha K. Levin and Maria Bruk Aupérin were a great boon in editing the final draft, while back in London, I must express a thanks to Claire Ward and the art team who did such a great job in designing the book, Miriam Rosenbloom and Gavin Morris, in particular. Last but far, far from least, I would like to thank Stephanie von Reiswitz for her wonderfully offbeat illustrations. They add enormously to the sense of fun that, I hope, permeates the book.

My final thanks must go to my family. My wife, Cilene, and young son, Thomas, were enthusiastic supporters throughout the research and writing phases, but I must single out my then eight-year-old daughter, Gabriella, for a special debt of gratitude. Fascinated from the beginning by the idea that animals could behave so strangely, she was at one point demanding a "silly new fact" to take to school each day. Each day I'd deliver a handful of candidates and each day she'd weigh them up. The editing skills she displayed in deciding a particular piece of information "wasn't funny enough" or, even more damning, "that everyone knows that" were pretty much flawless. No author should be without such a taskmaster driving him on. Thanks, Gabs. And I agree, the farting herring are my favorites, too.

—Augustus Brown, London

About the Author

Augustus Brown's fascination with the strange side of animal life began on a Welsh farm where he grew up surrounded by cows that could sense rain, highly combustible sheep, and chickens that could easily be hypnotized. In researching this book, he drew on decades of scientific archives, books and studies, scores of zoological and biological websites, and consulted leading experts in the animal science world. He lives in London with his wife and two children.